Revelation 12:1

And there appeared a woman clothed with the sun and the moon under her feet, and upon her head a crown of twelve stars.

The minister taught this verse in our self -improvement study guide titled "Who is God". As I read one of my poems, I thought about the Minister's guidance on this verse in reference to the moon was under her feet. He explained that this could represent the words of the prophets. I then began to remember an old gospel song that said, "we are standing on the promises of Jesus" In other words standing on his word. I began to think about how I had to stand on his word. The words of the Jesus in our midst. The power of this thought gave me the image on my book which is close to an image that I had before paying attention to this verse or studying the Ministers words pertaining to it. My artist's name is BlueRyse with a Blue moon rising in the background of my image as a logo. Well for this poetic journey that has been 13 years in the making, I finally have decided to stand on the moon. My blue moon that reminds me of being a Mary of today with the guidance of The Most Honorable Minister Louis Farrakhan.

Here's a picture of my logo BlueRyse which is now the inspiration for the cover of this book and the title. The only way to rise into Wisdom, would be to stand on the word. (moon)

ABOUT THE AUTHOR

The year is 2023 and I Jerri X have been on this earth for 51 beautiful years. My journey has been rough, but I wouldn't change anything. It was my journey that helped me grow into the woman that I am today. I used to cry about being an outcast in almost every group from school friends to churches. However, this was destined so that I would continue to seek the knowledge of God.

I'm not going to spend time on my entire bio since it is mentioned throughout this poetic journey. I will say that I have three beautiful daughters, five grandchildren, a beautiful husband and many family and friends. I'm not very close to most of my family as I would like to be but in time maybe I will be. After coming out of darkness, I was so excited to help others see, that they didn't want to see me coming. They would continue to chose a life in hell rather than hear someone that feels that they have peaked into Heaven. This is ironic since I wrote a novel about 10 years ago titled "I'd rather go to hell than the heaven that you're in". It was all about learning how to approach others that you want to go in the direction that you are going in, without causing them to choose the opposite which could lead them to doom. Well, I've learned to adjust and Shut Up unless I'm asked. I'm asked a lot of questions so I'm still talking but it's because they can see the change in my life (All praises due to Allah!)

This poetic journey tells the story of my life. Because of who I am today, I was reluctant to release this collection of poems that are over a decade old. But I think that it's important for many to understand my journey. I think that they should know where I came from. I will never stop learning but it is important to hear that I learned something over these years. My life is a beautiful story of a black lady rising into wisdom that saved her life. As you will read, she never stopped believing that she would have a wonderful husband which is very important for her success in life.

I have been a member of three churches but never got something that would change my life. I needed transformation. Because of the desire to obtain knowledge, I found the teachings from a man named Elijah

Muhammad that would transform my life. Today, I am healthier physically, mentally, and spiritually. I follow how to eat to live which is a book of guidance from God to Elijah Muhammad, which has me weighing less and I'm full of energy. I know how to relax and let go of anxiety, depression and anger which is a mental healing. This happens from following guidance to pray, fast and eat the right foods. I am healthier spiritually because I know who God is. I no longer look in the sky for a mystery God. I know him and that knowledge has me striving daily to do his will. That is how I can put my creation on paper and let those who can hear, hear what I have to say. So, who is this author? I am a woman who has been on a journey that was always meant for this purpose. I am nothing without God. And with him I am everything. There's nothing stopping me. The same can be for you. As you read my work, which at the beginning can get a little juicy(I used to be a hip-hop artist), you will hear the struggle and probably identify with much of it. I have just read some of my work again years later and I can identify the Ryse. Can you?

INTRODUCTION

This is a collection of poems that I have written over the course of 13 years. I start from the beginning which were written in 2008 to my current collection which were written in 2022. Back in 2008, as I was healing from a divorce, I began to have the Will to write my feelings on paper in poetic form. I would go on to start writing novels that stemmed from my poems, to plays, songs, and speeches. It was not until recently in my life that I decided to put my motivational thoughts into products and services that could potentially help others to Heal as I have Healed. My store is Blue Deals & Heals which got named from my artist's name Blueunique.

After starting my online store, I was bombarded with my own ideas. The Will to Deal & Heal became my overall motto and theme. The Will is when you bury your pride and come into the understanding that you must make a change in your life; to deal with all issues that keep you from being in an internal peaceful state of mind. When you get the will, you can start to deal, which is the action plan. This stage takes much discipline. When you become disciplined, you can push through all hardships. After pushing through, you are healed. Will there be more hardships? Yes! But you now have developed the formula and can always have the will to deal & heal.

I am going to start with The Will which is best described in my earlier poems dating back to 2008. I will then start Dealing which is somewhere between 2012 and 2018. The Healing chapter will be short since my healing has just begun. In 2020 after becoming in submission with Allah, I developed a disciplined way of life, and I received a powerful gift. I am on the path to being healed physically, mentally, and spiritually.

In conclusion, I will talk about BlueRyse which is my current artistic name. I write more songs than I do poetry as I learned to communicate in the blue energy. In Dec. of 2022 I wrote the song titled BlueRyse. This song is written in poetry form.

PART 1

THE WILL

She Got Issues (2008)

My name is Jerri Locke Coleman Williams I was born October the 8th 1971 in Chicago IL. Shortly after I was born, my mother and I returned home to the little town of Tamms, Illinois. I guess you could say that I lived in Tamms all my life. I did experience some city life while in college for four years. I am a proud mother of three daughters Lakeisha Johnson, Corika Coleman and Shawnjera Locke. They are my world, and they are also my biggest issue in life. I am currently single. I have been married twice. My first marriage was at an early age of 22 I didn't want to have a second child out of wedlock so marriage it was. After the husband finished his five years prison sentence, we could not seem to pick up the pieces. Then finally I thought I met my dream, my second husband. After some tough years and unbearable disappointments, we parted ways. Well! Actually! He just left. Anyway, God makes no mistakes here I am single but thriving and full of life.

Lakeshia, my first born, is 25. She has three beautiful children. Making me a young good- looking granny. Lakeisha has a gift that is so rare. Wherever she goes, she shines. She can light up a room that's consumed with darkness. You may think you hate her when she walks in, but before she leaves, you will love her. She was full of strength the day she was born. I remembered the doctor gasping for air as she pulled his stethoscope 2 minutes after entering this world. She had two teeth by the time she was two months old Anne was running at about 10 months old. At the age of 5, she was giving me advice and telling me that she had saved money to help me with our bills. I used to cry about being broke all the time one day she said it to me, "Momma! if you keep saying you broke, then you will always be.

Think positive." I still use her advice. I love this girl who is now a woman. She is definitely an image of me. She looks like me. She talks like me. She even walks like me. At least two times a week, I am mistaken for my own daughter. I know it is a compliment; but it is also a constant reminder of her being so disappointed in me. You see, to her, I can do nothing right. She swears that I was not a good mother to her. She doesn't just come out and say that either; she gets determined to embarrass me by constant ridicule. For years add cry, quotation mark Lord help me to get through to her, I did take care of her. I used to cry so hard, when she would say, "you have an issue Momma. You are not perfect." I wrestled with this over, and over again. I prayed about it and meditated. Then one day, I received my revelation." Yes! Keisha, I have an issue; but the issue is loving you. The issue is trying to please you. The issue is trying to prove myself to you. Knowing that it's never enough, will make anyone have an issue. If my issue is drugs, you would make me overdose. If my issue is alcohol, you will make me ruin my liver. If my issue is food, then I will get big as a house. So, you are the issue."

Corika, my second daughter, is 18. Praise God, she has no children yet. I'm not very good at being a grandparent. I need to retire and have all grown kids. Coco is a lot like Keisha, but they seem like they are from two different worlds. Although Keisha was rough to raise, she was always compassionate. Coco thinks the universe revolves around her. I take the blame for this. You see, after watching Keisha go through her teenager years, I had labeled myself as a filling parent. Since coco's father was not going to be in the picture, I decided to make sure that she felt like one parent was enough. I was older and had more money, so I tried to give her even more than I was able to give Keisha. Everyone called her spoiled. Maybe she was but like Keisha, she complains that it wasn't enough. Keisha didn't complain much until she was grown. However, Coco can cause me to jump through hoops to give her what she wants and still tell me the next day that she's mad because I should have had her buy a better daddy so she wouldn't be broke. And every now and then she also says so she wouldn't be dark skin. This really hurts because I think she is beautiful.

For some reason, black families 10 to down those that are different than they are. Maybe they were only playing, but it affects people, nevertheless. Coco was always called dark skin playful names. As her mother, I made sure that she was over poured with compliments and the best hair staff. This issue was so close to my heart, that I often cry and became furious. I remember when Coco was three years old. I had bought her a beautiful hat to take pictures. She cried that she couldn't wear a hat. When I asked why, she said, "big head Coco. Big head Coco." I was so mad. Come to find out, some idiot in my family was calling my 3-year-old big headed. At least, they waited until she was older to call her other things. Then when she became older and had listened to me and held her head high, she was down for thinking she too cute.

I am so proud of Coco. Despite everything, she has been excellent in school. She is a math whiz. I have never been able to accomplish what she has. I am convinced that she's going to make something of herself. She has also been downed because she has the confidence that she will be whatever she wants if she tries. I remember sitting there listening to a couple of people tell her that just because you go to college, does not mean you are going to be anything or get a job. She replied with a statement that made me the proudest mother ever, "well, I'll keep trying until I do. I'll further my education. I'll go where jobs are." They continued to try and convince her that it may not happen. I then stepped in and spoke for her. I told them that it is up to us adults to help her know her dreams are attainable rather than making her feel that she will not be able to make it in this big bad world. I wonder if they knew that their attitudes could cause so many young women in our family to have an issue.

I've basically created a diva that's causing me all kinds of issues. We have gotten used to eating hamburger helper, so does she can have all the extra money. I give to her, and she don't seem to realize it. Keisha always driven the men away from me; where Coco wants them to stay so she can get some of their pay. Well, you know what I mean, they can help freeing up more for her. I sometimes wonder if she loves anyone. No one would guess but Coco is much harder than Keisha. You can get through to Keisha's heart. Coco has a brick wall up and ask her mother it drives me crazy to not be able to find the key. Everyone reminds me that she will get better when she gets grown. I guess I'm just sensitive. I need my girls to love me now. I love them more than anything in this world. I love them more than I love myself. I need for them to understand the sacrifice that I've made to ensure that they are provided for. For them to ignore me and watch me suffer, is an issue.

Shawnjera is my baby. She is only 6 and she is still sweet. However, I know she's going to be the worst one of all because she is spoiled. I really don't care what she does to me. I'll be thankful to just get to see her grow up. I was kind of old having her. 35 to be exact. It is true when they say you are too old to be having kids. This little girl runs our house. She tells me and Coco what to do and we obey. She is so cute she is irresistible I am thankful that Coco loves her and helps me take care of her. She is different than the other kids in our family. While they are out playing an acting grown up, she would rather sing and play with toys. I am thankful that she is different I believe that is Gods way of showing me a different way. I love her so much that it ****** me off when I hear people putting her down because they think they have figured out the difference. One of my family members once said that she couldn't talk Anne had less sense than a 2-year-old. I was upset and tried to prove otherwise. Vengeance is mine said the Lord. I had to remember that he will prove it he did and if I continue to trust him, I know that he will continue.

I never imagined having another child after my first 2; but I met the one that I thought was the one, got married and then pregnant. It felt good to be pregnant and not ashamed to be. Well, everything seemed to be coming together and to top it off it was a boy. Well God had another plan. I lost my son at 36 weeks pregnant. It is still a mystery. But I tried not to think about it; because a couple of years later, I was blessed with another girl. I was so mad when they said she was a girl. I should have been thanking the Lord, but instead I was too busy being selfish. I thought I needed to replace my son. Anyway, before she was born, I found out that she would only have one kidney. Again, I became angry instead of having faith. I did pray and I received grace. She was born healthy with no kidney disease. One kidney didn't form but she could live fine with one. She came into this world and started touching lives with her beautiful voice. One day I hope she will be thankful for her gift of music; For now, I am grateful. She was less than one year old and saying every song she heard on the radio. Her words weren't that clear then, but she had the melody down. She even has started to rap now. I guess she's following in my footsteps.

When Shawnjera's daddy left us, I began to question God all over again. I knew he loved our little girl; But I wondered if maybe she or I wasn't enough to keep him. I guess he couldn't get over the loss of our son. He did cry often. I never cried again once I laid eyes on my baby girl. I knew that God planned for her to be here with me. Right now, in my life, I get weakened by those older girls, and my baby shows me that she loves me more than anything. I know that I have years of issues to come with her; but I'm ready; three times is a charm. I know that I won't strike out. I am a winner.

Keisha, you are so right. Your momma has issues. You have told everyone, "She got issues". Now it is my turn to tell the world what I think about my issues there is issues and your issues. As you read, ask yourself. Can you work out your biggest issue? Will you even admit that you have issues? So, I have an issue. Can you love me through my issue?

I'M FREE

Child, why are you wearing that? People gone think you a slut.

Everybody don't want to see your big butt.

If you keep doing what you do, you won't get out of your rut.

The way you raise your kids is all wrong.

Maybe they will respect you if you weren't in the club all night long.

We heard dance like a stripper is your favorite song.

You got the nerve to go to church with your head high, unto our Lord you cry.

The way you get around. No smiles your way. All you get is a frown.

Just who do you think you are? Walking around like you a star.

Everywhere you go you shine.

You're nothing, we know you drink too much wine.

Who cares if you have always been kind.

What's the matter with you? Everybody gone say you crazy.

Saying whatever you want to. Well, that's how Liz raised me.

I'm 4 x 9 so I do what I want to do.

She said it's gone be alright. All my life I had to fight.

When you stop worrying if man is wrong or right.

You will figure out how to receive your site.

My heart is filled with peace.

Praise God I'm free.

11

Issues

Liz is my maternal grandmother. She lived an expiring life. Throughout her life, she taught her kids and grandkids about things they would face in the world. I've always had a problem with being judged by those who felt like they were doing so right. She believed that once you were grown, some people needed to leave you alone. All her wisdom and strength became a part of me. I realized that only God could judge me. I made peace with the enemy. My heart was filled with love and peace. Now I am free.

You may look or act different than those around you. Don't worry the Bible says that God loves you. So, don't give up on doing what's right, because you fell short at times. Always be yourself. Remember that tomorrow is a new day. Learn how to forgive those that seem to be against you. Don't stay trapped in the conspiracy of misery. And you will be free.

WALK THE WALK

I talked to talk.

My ego grown tall like Jack in the Beanstalk.

I feel like I can have it all and you can't stop me.

If you try hater, I pray you will live to see.

Success describes who I be.

I talk in riddles but always understand.

There is no secret to God's plan.

I can talk until I'm blue in the face.

But when he says move I must at his pace.

Can I talk myself through this race?

I know I've done wrong, but please let me plead my case.

Now shut up girl don't you hear me talking? What's wrong with you?

Can't you hear me? I'm trying to tell you time is near.

Don't you hear what I'm saying?

Come back child. I'm not playing.

Why don't anyone here?

Why don't they fear?

I've done talked and talked.

But did I walk the walk?

Issue

What good is it to know everything, but no one listens? Maybe you should go another route. While you're talking, how are you walking? Let your light shine. It is hard to see in the dark period what is done in the dark comes to the light. So, do right and it will be easier to tell someone about the light.

The issue has been difficult for me to grasp, I know that I'm telling the truth. Why aren't they listening? Do as I say, not as I do. Was a phrase often used but is a contradiction. Most kids and adults learn better by seeing rather than hearing. I used to have an issue with trying to tell my kids what to do. They often would ask, what did you use to do? I felt like my head would explode at times. Why can't they understand that I'm telling them, so they won't make the same mistakes? I pray for answers. I have been given them repeatedly. Change begins with me. If I keep doing right, my girls will eventually open their eyes.

My most recent issue has been with A man. I want him to be right. I feel that he can be the one, so he can't be out there doing things that are wrong. Yes, I'm going to fuss until he quits; However, he may quit me. I can be stubborn at times, but I'm trying to take advice. From one woman to another, she told me to walk the Christian walk and he will eventually follow. Can I do this? Pray and shut up. I think I can. I have always had a problem with talking too much. However, If I keep my walking pace, I won't have to talk so much, I'll be out of breath.

THE STAGE

Can you let me on the stage?

Is it my age?

Or that I'm full of rage?

Can you turn the page?

Or let me out this freaking cage?

Do you know how to read me?

If not ninja unleash me!

Gotta gets this hood out of my system.

Ninja too nice, I'll mess around and diss him.

Time to pull the cord.

Gotta goes to church tomorrow.

Can't give up now because he bought me too far.

Can you get off the stage?

Will we sway?

When your music play?

Will you pass the Mike my way?

You're wrapping the same old ish?

How much money you are getting.

And how many women you are sleeping with.

As you can see anybody can rhyme.

Step off the stage and let me shine.

No matter the size.

I'm ready to rise.

While you stay here.

I'll Conquer the skies.

Willing to move to the next phase.

Been waiting on this moment all my days.

My rage has gone away with age.

You let me out the cage, by turning the page.

You unleashed me. Now read me.

Give me my stage.

Issue

The small -town rappers are hilarious. All of them chasing quick fame. Whenever I throw some ideas their way, I'm shut down or ignored. They whisper, "she too old and crazy." I'm not ready to give up on my dream. So, I'm building my own stage. If you're close minded. You don't have to rock to my beat. This is a new beat. On a new stage. If you are performer, you can at any age.

Earlier this year, I was having a conversation about being a rapper with my oldest daughter and our friend. Someone suggested that I should continue to pursue my rapping career. When I presented the idea to them, I was shut down. Her exact words were, "stick with your poems". After wrestling with this, I confronted them. I was told that as an older woman, I make bad choices. In other words, you are too old to pursue your dreams. She then states that she just trying to give me constructive criticism. I strongly disagree. If I become successful, then everyone is bragging and happy. If I fail, they are doing the same. I kept wrestling with this repeatedly, when one day while listening to Brandy, the R&B artist, I heard my confirmation period she stated that a rapper that helped her with one of her songs was an excellent poet. I began to laugh because this rapper was not young. Guess it doesn't matter how old he is.

Sometimes people self- worthy words can stop you in your tracks. Be careful who you listen to. If what they are telling you doesn't push you forward, most likely you should just smile and walk away. It is amazing how many people never get on the stage because someone is holding them back. Well, I've been held back too long. I'm going to push you out of my way; If you are blocking my walkway to my stage.

SCHEMING

Sitting on the block,
tired but waiting on my dollars to flock.
Unfortunately, God moving the Clock.
Ninja, you running out of time.
Come on Lord, slow down, I'm trying to get my grind.
On, in these streets. It's not my fault. These ninjas pheaning.
I hate it. But money makes me. I'm scheming.
I may sell you a rock.
Literally from the dirt. The real **** is in my sock.
There is more money to be made more women to be laid.
and if they are scheming, I'll stay paid
scheme until I die.
No matter how many cries.
I know the truth but rather live a lie.
Doing wrong is easier than doing right.
I may have to try.
How long can I live this way?
When is my day to face him what will I say?
Now are you ready to receive your pay?
I don't think so because he doesn’t play.
So, here's your chance. Get right. Stop dreaming.
No one gets a free ride to glory.
By days of scheming.

Issue

Fast money is the root to all evil. Some of us believe that if a person has a lot of money, then they are doing so well in life. Money can't buy happiness. It won't get you into heaven. Having money is nice, but get it in the right way, then you won't have to do so many horrible simple things to get it. I don't know about y'all, but when I have a guilty conscious, I feel horrible, and all stressed out. Stress is a killer, so, doing things right, will make life less stressful.

Have you ever been around a person that has different moods depending on how much money they have? Well, I have come an I used to be one of them. I'm trying to break myself from it but sometimes I still get that way. I don't want to be like those people who can't smile nor hold their head up if they are broke. Now it's not their fault, society has categorized people by their financial worth. If you bring a new man home and he has less money than your ex, he just will not be good enough. How many of us stick with a no- good person because they have money? Not me, I have never been in love with the money having dudes. I always felt that if he had the best car, then he had too many women. I know, I was being prejudiced, but oh well I had to follow my gut.

I like nice things, but I can do without. I love having a Peace of Mind even more. I have always said, I would take a fast- food working man over one that does anything and anybody for money. God will bless a little to be a lot and a lot to be a little. I know from experience. When I was younger, I had money coming left and right. I thought I was so happy. Years later, I began to look around and wonder where did my money go? I have nothing to show for it. I bought a couple of things, but I was making way more than that. Where is it? It wasn't blessed so it was taken. I was so blind that I did not see where it went. When I gave up the paper chase, I received my site and found true happiness.

JOGGED THE LAST MILE

Your destination may be the bench.
Mine is the finish line.
I'm not worried about the time.
We all have our own individual deadline.
I believe my time is set.
I'm willing to wager all I got on this final bet.
I know there's something left in his life for me.
Maybe, I will be, a pulsating vessel for him to use, so that you can see.
If you quit, I'll keep going.

Even If it takes all night, then there is morning.
I continued to fight. I want to win at this game called life.
I'm always wrong, hardly ever right.
Thank God. When he created night.
He also created daylight.
So, when I make a wrong turn.
No matter the burn.
I'm steered back on the road.
I've been showed.
Lesson learned.
Thank God I continue to try.
My destination somewhere in the Sky.

Don't need no drugs to get me high.

No booze to make me sigh.

No man to make me cry.

No one to ask me why.

Or make me say my.

I will do this even if I must do it alone.

With God by my side, I have grown.

Thank you, God, for this beautiful, grateful, peaceful, forgiving, loving smile as I jogged the last mile.

Issue

I'm always on some new diet or workout plan. Since nothing seems to work well, I constantly feel like giving up. Although, I know that I didn't complete the diet nor be consistent with workout, I expect instant results. It wasn't until I learned to be thankful for the ability to try, that I accept it today and looked forward to tomorrow. Sometimes I find myself being caught up in a web of negative people that make me feel like everything I do is for nothing. I don't know why they got to me, but they did. I found myself doing what they did just to fit in. Eventually, I felt drained and negative also. I began to look at others that were trying to move forward with jealousy. Mainly, because I didn't have the desire to fix what was wrong with me. No! looks may not be everything, but I don't like it when I look like crap. I also feel like crap. How can I help others if I can't help myself? So, I decided, you may stop but I can't. God gave me another chance every day and I'm going to make the best out of it. I believe that one day, I can run further. When I get to my last mile, I will smile and be thankful that I had the motivation to run this mile.

BLACK QUEEN

She moving.

She moving.

The way her body sway.

She may be a star someday.

Born a Queen but by the time she was weaned,

inherit the curse they could conquer her dreams.

She cried out they stole my King.

Who stole your king?

Her eyes were blue. Who?

They put him in an orange suit and took away his shoes.

Who?

We all know who. The question is why?

You talk too much.

You are a nag.

You're mean.

It's the curse of the black Queen.

Why does she act this way?

Still don't know what to do or say.

To keep her King strong. Don't go away.

She began to realize no man will stay,

as long as she did things her way.

If you're looking for me now, I'm in the closet where I will pray.

"Lord my human King has gone astray I'm prepared to meet my everlasting King one day.

My hair is nappy, my mouth is big,

I even like wearing wigs, but my grave you will not help dig.

I will always love you my earthly King.

but to the heavens I sing I need to be redeemed.

Lord take your black Queen

Issue

For years, I've heard of the generational curse of black women. It's the reason why we can't keep a man. The reason why we can't keep best friends. It's the reason why our daughters hate us. Well, this may very well be true. However, I believe that understanding the curse can help us move forward. There are so many good sides to the curse that we can't see because we've been stereotyped as this evil woman. Black women remember why you must be strong. Whose black men fill the prisons? Well, there went our Kings. We cry, but most of us learned how to pray even harder so we wiped the tears away and decided that even though I was taught not to work, I can't let the kids starve, the need they need clothes, and if I get good at this, I may be able to help them go to college period now we're getting smart. When we get a new man, he came run us. We make our own money and decisions. We would love for him to take the head again, but what do we do when he leaves. Therefore, as a black Queen, we stay in the League. We know what he going to say before he even let it out. Woman I'm leaving you, you talk too much, you are nag, you are mean. Let's tell them that it's ok. I'll continue to pray that I meet a real man one day. As for a King, I'll stick with Jesus. Oh, what a day it will be, when this black Queen receives her throne in glory. Be proud you black Queens that you were able to raise their babies on your own. Be proud that where he was weak you were strong. Remember the devil comes after those he fears will be strong for Jesus. So, stay in your closets praying. My King, my heavenly King, have mercy on this black Queen.

PRETTY

Can we talk?

I like the way it feels when this boy touches me.

I know I'm young but why do I feel all tingly?

Especially when his deep voice says you so pretty.

One day I may take you to the big city.

Buy you some pretty clothes and change your name to Kitty.

I've always wanted to look pretty.

Those folks in the small town just didn't get me.

When the boys came around, I walked with A twist.

Sit down girl before you get that itch.

That's what the little fast girls get when they try to switch.

Can we talk?

I know you're not talking about that Boo?

Is not talked about under my roof, it's taboo.

Too many watermelon seeds is the reason her belly grew.

Who is the daddy? I don't know. I talked to a few.

But who did you do?

Do what? That's taboo.

I tried talking to you.

Can we talk?

I don't like the way it feels when he touches me.

It hurts and the pain is felt deeply.

When it's over he gets up and leaves me.

I feel so ugly downright filthy.

Should I feel so alone there is no one with me.

Can we talk? I Feel the itch, I feel the Burn.

Why didn't you talk to me, I could have learned.

When you were cursing and wore a permanent frown?

Why didn't you tell me that it was this that had you down?

Is this why you didn't call me pretty?

Were you afraid that I would be the next Kitty?

Is this why my skirts had to be long, and I couldn't wear short shorts?

My hair style was ugly, and we grew apart?

Can we talk?

This has the end.

Can you accept where I've been and become my friend?

Even if I became Kitty?

I'm yours so am I pretty?

Issue

Pretty is a strong adjective. What female doesn't love being pretty? Whether it's their face, body, hair, our belongings, the goal is to still be pretty. Some of us was unfortunate enough to be called or considered pretty by our loved ones. Perhaps, they didn't feel pretty themselves. Anyway, we began to search. There has to be someone out there in that big world, who thinks I'm pretty? If only I knew, I was pretty, I may not have to search for confirmation. I tried talking about it, but no one seemed to understand. They acted as if they never went through these things. Well, I guess I'm crazy. That's what I need to talk about. I feel so messed up inside. I found someone to tell me I'm pretty but now I feel uglier than ever. The world is spinning too fast. I don't know what to do. Someone! Help me. I need someone to talk to.

FREAKS COME OUT AT NIGHT

When I was 10, I was a size 2.

So, how could I be a Dallas cowboy cheerleader like you?

Maybe a stripper in the hood clubs and work the night shift too.

You a brick house, you thick. You the type of girl we love to get with.

That junk in your trunk is alright.

Will I see you at the club tonight?

I'll be there on the flow, dropping it low.

Got this dress that hugs my big Bud tight.

It's alright, I can wear it 'cause freaks come out at night.

These women sit down when the lights come on.

Insecure of her roles are don't want a bone threatened that she may lose her happy home.

Maybe if I lose 10 pounds,

I can walk around,

With shorts shorts on and make those that love me frown.

I want them to love me

So, when I see them coming and I'm dressed inappropriately,

I'll hide my cleavage by folding my arms.

And walk sideways so the width of my hips caused no harm.

I'll keep my head down my night life flashes are still on.

I'm confused, why can she look that way?

Is it because she's bright like day?

Gone girl, master will come fetch you when is night to play.

Is this why they say what they say?

And make us feel we're good for nothing but on our backs we lay.

No not doing the day nor turn on the lights.

You can't see me. I'm just a freak of the night.

Stop living back in those days.

Connect with your daughters, don't lose them in this maze. Give them some praise.

Tell them, I love you, you are beautiful. Instill in them why they are raised.

Maybe they won't be ashamed.

And you will see what goes on with their hearts, minds, and bodies, with no one to blame.

Teach them you are a beautiful sight.

You have the right to dance and dress in what you like in broad daylight.

This is a new day.

We will not be the freaks that come out at night.

Issue

Our culture, African Americans, tend to be so close minded and judgmental when it comes to our sisters. We have been taught to cover ourselves so that we will not tempt men. I can understand that, but what I can't understand is why women of other races can walk around gorgeous and not be considered a ****. We can't be on underwear commercials unless we happen to be shapeless. We can be on television just not shows that everyone watches. Were considered X rated. I think since we've been stereotyped for so long, some of us decided to live up to this role. We rarely know that we are beautiful. So, we seek someone to help us feel beautiful. Most of the time it's at the nightclub. Nightlife is a wonderful place for us. We can be as beautiful and thick as we please and I guarantee somebody gonna like me.

CAN YOU HEAR ME NOW?

Can you hear me now?

I said it loud, 'cause I was proud.

Never ashamed of the words that flowed my mouth.

Those that felt me,

can relate to what my big cousin saying about me.

Sometimes, I walked away ignoring what he had to say.

Little did I know he had no time to waste.

See we don't know when it's our big day.

So, say what you got to say.

I'll do it.

I wrote this for you boy.

You remind me of me.

I can hear you now, “say it unique.”

It wasn't only you that stood out in a crowd.

I was also labeled, “dang that girl loud.”

Anyway, I learned a lesson from you. Speak loud and speak proud.

You may not always be around.

Who knew that the sound of your unique voice, could no longer be found?

Unless we keep it in our hearts.

Then our family may never fall apart.

How many of us can live our lives today?

and say what we want to say?

Like Shay Shay.

Well, I think I know what he would say today (laughing loud) “please don't frown?

I love y'all. Can you hear me now?”

Issue

My cousin Shay Shay passed away at 30 years of age. He left an impression on me that I would carry my entire life. Say it now, while you can. Also, to watch how we treat others. Maybe they just needed an ear or shoulder to cry on. What if you were the last one to be given that honor? Will you say something to help the other person, or something to uplift and make them feel better? Will you be able to say I love you from the bottom of your heart? Will it be too late? Because he can’t hear us now?

HER ISSUE

You are about to read a poem about my maternal grandmother. She was a bad woman. I don't know if there was anything that she could not do. When she passed away, she left a lot of memories. She was such a legend. People around our town still frequently used her hilarious but inspirational terminology.

You wanted to run away at times? "Gone boy, you got diamonds in your back you look better going then you look coming".

You called someone fat? "Don"t nothing but a dog won't a bone. I'm a big fat woman with meat shaking on my bones every time I shake, a skinny woman lose her home".

You thought you knew it all? "Girl, you going around the teapot trying to find the handle."

Don't even try being the boss. "I'm 3 x 9 ain't got nobody to mind."

Granny that girl trying to fight me saying that's her boyfriend. "Tell her, he a much right man. He got just as much right to be yours, as he has to be hers.

You didn't do what she said? "Child you must not believe fat meat greasy."

Now when she got mad, she got more- funny and these ain't curse words. "

Kiss what you twist and not my wrist."

She couldn't stand for you to lie. "You a lying sack of **** and your nickname is Doo Doo."

SHE BADDDD

This mother was bad.

Always wore a bad hat with shoes to match.

To church she went but never wore flats.

She dressed in a bad suit that matched her hat

and on the mothers bent she sat.

She mothered with pride with God on her side.

She lived for him so to you she had nothing to hide.

Just when did she get tired?

With 14 kids and 200 and something grandkids, she was so admired.

Even though she done things or said that we didn't like,

you must admit when you grew up you realized that she was right.

I don't remember too many sad days.

I do remember how much she prayed and whip me if I misbehaved.

Then we laughed and watched her dance to disco lady.

I still can't explain to this day, how I smelt her soulful cooking 100 feet away.

Y'all may think I'm crazy,

but every time I feel lazy,

I think of this woman who was so amazing.

Nowadays if our baby is crying,

we rushed him to the hospital like they dying.

She used to give them roots out the yard and they were fine.

I saw it with my own eyes y'all, I'm not lying.

Sometimes missing her I get sad.

Then I dream that Michael Jackson moonwalking around her in heaven singing'
"she bad she bad you know it."

Not for all you judging people, that means she's all good.

This is written by the girl who is still a little hood.

My momma, myself, and my daughters we are her.

We look like her, we talk like her, we walked like her, we are her.

We may not be perfect, but we been raised to be a mother by her.

She was known for her comical sayings.

All inspirational but you all know she was just playing.

This woman is a legend. She bad.

Sometimes she got downright mad.

Most of all, she was the best mother ever to be had.

She Bad.

PICKING GREENS

The constant aches have made me cold.

His deceit has punctured my soul.

Why do I put myself through this? I'm getting too old.

Iit's a cycle of pain over and over again.

Now I sit ashamed, waiting on the world to end.

Who is that knocking at my door?

Might as well leave, I'm coming out no more.

I'm a disgrace.

How can I ever show my face?

Come on child, we picking greens today.

I look, it's Nana Sis. And the crew. Dang there's no getting away.

I wish I could be disobedient today.

Hey Jerri Boo, you ready?

"I'm too cute to get all sweaty.

I'm coming, they gone see that I've been crying.

I'm OK, child stop lying.

Come on time to pick some greens.

Dang I still have on my true religion jeans.

Here's your knife.

Then she plopped over and cut them wild greens with one swipe.

I couldn't reach the plant my jeans were too tight.

Sorry nana, I know you see my Crack.

That's OK girl. Get you some greens and your dignity back.

You look good. When I was young like you, I wore my clothes tight too.

I was a hot Mama in them Wrangler jeans.

I just didn't wear them to pick greens.

We picked greens all the time back in the day.

You see Mama didn't play.

If you ate, then you helped fetch and prepare what was on your plate.

Dinner was never late.

Got ham hocks boiling. I'm putting fat back in mine.

I got some oxtails for the youngsters that eat no swine.

I'm getting hungry I haven't eaten all day.

Been too sad. Well child did you pray?

Do you know how to pray?

First repent for those sins you know and don't know that you done today.

And mean it I say.

Then watch as the blessings come your way.

Everything will be fine.

My God is always on time.

When we get back to the house, stick around for a few.

I'm gonna tell you what your Papa used to do.

Believe me everything that happens to you,

big momma already done went through.

Well why did you stay, if he was that way?

I prayed every day and kept faith that things will be OK.

Now hold your head up Stop looking mean.

Get in there and fix the hot water cornbread to go with the greens.

Issue

Nana Sis. and the crew consisted of my paternal grandma and her sisters. When you least expected it, they would show up and make you go to the green Patch. I used to think it was just about picking greens, but as I grew, I realized that they were getting me out the house to share some wisdom. I am so thankful for the wisdom and for making me the best wild turnip green cooker in the area. I used to boil them greens to death, and they were still tough. No matter how much salt I put in them, they didn't taste right. One day I was eating some of Aunt Dora's greens and wondered why they taste so good. Aunt Dora was my grandma's oldest sister. She was a pro at cooking wild turnip greens. I'm still using her recipe to this day. She said baby you got to cook the greens for a while before you put the season in there. Add some fat meat grease too and that will tender them babies right on up. Then take your fingers and squeeze your cornbread in with the greens. No one used Forks to eat greens at Aunt Dora's.

HIS ISSUE

As you read this poem, ask yourself, where are they trying to get to? My grandpa was a legend. He will be talked about for many years to come. I chose a few of the many stories told of him for this poem. First, how he was called Ping Pong Pete. Second, he was called Big John. Last, everyone called him Big Unc. I could have gone on and on about this man. When he was alive, I wasn't discouraged by much. His work ethics alone helped mold me into the woman that I am today. Also, in this poem I point out of few more important parts of the fish fry. Aunt Rene, one of my grandma’s sisters, has always been one of the best women on this earth. She is the only sister left. She been passing out juicy fruit gum to generations of kids. She believed that kids needed something sweet to chew on and maybe they will grow to be a sweet grown up. Next, I mentioned the competitive daughters. My daddy's three sisters were amazing and so very-different. All three loved to cook. I hated choosing which cake taste better. I love them all, but they made me pick. Then there's the prideful sons that bickered. They all wanted to please grandpa by proving one new more than the other. You haven't had fish until it’s cooked in his big black pot. We still have that pot. The barn is gone, the shade tree gone, but we can't lose the pot.

Fish fry

It was the last Saturday in May.

Time to prepare for the biggest fish fry, just like the ones back in the day.

People came from miles away.

To gather at the old born and eat fish all day.

The women sat under the tree.

And took turns cranking the handle to the homemade ice cream.

The children played and smacked on juicy fruit from main train.

The competitive daughters couldn't take the heat.

They stayed in to make the sweets.

When they finished the cakes, they were too neat to eat.

At the barn all you heard was laughter.

As the men drank beer and bragged about whose car was faster.

In the background, the prideful sons bickered.

About things such as, who can get the fish done quicker,

which wood burns better under the pot,

and that habanero Peppers were not that hot.

That reminds me, I forgot to put Peppers on my list.

Gotta have hot pepper and onion to go with fish.

Time to go on my journey. I have a long list.

It must be complete to fulfill his wish.

If this fish fry is to be a success,

it must be better than all the rest.

Almost out the door when I heard him yell

“you gone yet GAIL?”

“Don't forget the red- hot sauce. That other **** too cheap. It is watered down. Red hot is what I eat.

Well, here I go.

I made it a mile down the road.

I see this man walking. I gotta stop, he too old.

Hey Sir, where are you going?

I'm going to a fish fry.

What fish fry?

Well, it's this friend of mine, we call him Ping Pong Pete. He's some kind of man.

I love watching little fish bones slide out the sides of his teeth.

One day he said he would teach me.

I just don't know if I will ever learn.

I think you can.

Put your faith in God not man.

Bye, I’ll see you at the fish fry.

I'm not stopping anymore.

I must get to this store.

Right before my eyes,

A young lady cries,

“Please stop I need a ride.”

Where are you going? To a fish fry

where my granddaddy told me of this man.

Big John they called him. He can pick a man up off his feet with one hand.

That sounds familiar where did he live?

Did he also pick up an automobile?

I have a boyfriend that beats me and won't let me sleep.

I was hoping Big John will take care of that creep.

Well, I guess, but I know a man,

that the presence of his hand

will protect you and guide you through this land.

Anyway, hop in. I have a feeling; you are going to the place where I've been.

Now I'm speeding. No more stops.

Look in the mirror. There is a freaking cop.

Lord, don't let him pull me over.

I have no money; I'm a single mother.

Ma'am, why are you driving so fast? Was I? I guess I'm anxious to get to this fish fry.

What fish fry?

Well, you see my Grandfather Big Leroy passed away,

but brought all this fish and froze it to be cooked on this day.

I'm his first grandchild and it's up to me to keep his legacy alive.

I was running late so faster I drive.

Wait a minute. Did you say Big Leroy? That's Big Unc. I heard about him.

My grandpa used to go hogging with him.

He said that Big Unc would go underwater and come back up with fish in every pocket, fish in his boots, and held his cigar with one tooth. Everyone look amazed; How does he do that trick? (In Unison) "His cigar is still lit".

Well gone, I hope everything goes well.

I'll send you your ticket in the Mail.

How about I finish my list

and you can get some fish.

OK yo ticket is dismissed.

Everything is complete.

I feel joy from the top of my head to the soles of my feet.

You tried devil but you didn't stop me.

Look at all these people gathered here to eat.

Listen up everybody there is plenty of food.

Enjoy yourself like grandpa would do.

This is a beautiful sight.

All the memories allow his legacy to be passed on tonight.

I think we can all use the man that kept him strong in our life.

So, let's prepare ourselves for the final fish fry.

The one in the Sky.

Let's start by giving praise to he, that sits high.

I can hear PaPa saying what the good book said

"You my Lord and savior that fed,

a multitude with two fish and five loaves of bread."

Issue

Did you figure out the destination? The final fish fry in the Sky. When we face our big day will we be ready? Will we have good stories told of us? Beautiful

SPEAK

Did I sleep with you last night?
Oh, hey! That's right baby I live by faith not by sight.
The way you treat others that you come across in life,
depends on your belief that everything is alright.
When things aren't going your way,
a thoughtful greeting like “how was your day?”
May not make everything OK,
but it surely beats a hateful greeting with nothing good to say.
So, when I walk up in a crowd,
and yeah! I speak loudly.
I love making the old folks proud.
That little girl is so sweet.
No matter what they say about her,
she always SPEAKS!

Issue

When I was growing up, if we walked in a house, we said hello or else my grandma stopped you and asked if you slept with her last night? If the answer was no, "Then why didn't you speak?" I used to think these old folks were crazy, but as I began to grow up, I understood how important greeting or speaking is. Just like everything else, it will become a thing of the past period there are many societies now that look at you crazy if you say hello. Well, I'm going to continue to speak. My grandma was very- proud of the woman she raised me to be. The world will move smoother, if more people are friendly. It's easier to smile and greet, than to frown and not speak.

OKIE DOKIE

Okie Dokie was a sweet way of this man saying OK.

Hey PA, can I go play? Okie Dokie, just don't stay late.

Hey PA, I got in trouble at school. Okie Dokie, next time follow the rules.

If not, I hate to, but you know what I'll use.

Hey Sir, I know you have a lot of kids, but can I have a bowl of rice?

Okie Dokie. There's plenty, and he didn't think twice.

He learned a long time ago how to sacrifice.

How to thank God, for what he put on the table.

And for letting him work as long as he was able.

Always keeping his family sheltered from the rain.

I heard that he was so thankful, that through the pain, he rarely complained.

Well thanks again old friend.

The rice was good and sweet.

Thanks for the encouragement you gave me.

Okie Dokie

Issue

I was very- young when this sweet man, my maternal grandpa, passed away. He was one of the good men back in his day. I can only imagine loving and caring for 14 kids. I only remember peace. I don't remember any cries of hunger. He had faith that everything would be OK. So, Okie Dokie was a phrase that he commonly used throughout the day. This world was so powerful that it stuck in my heart. I hope that I can become the woman that he would expect for me to be and use his phrase with sincerity.

My favorite memory of him, would be the time when he tricked me. I was only four years old period it was a normal school morning an mother has sent me

My favorite memory of him would be the time that he tricked me. I was only around four years old. It was a typical school morning in which I was sent across the yard to his house to catch the bus. The big problem was this ugly Brown dress that she made me wear. When I got there, I sat on his lap and said," I don't have to go to school today I'm sick." "Okie Dokie" he replied. Well, I was happy. "I'm gone spend the day with him and not be seen by the kids in this ugly dress." Well, the bus pulled up. "Time to get on the bus Jer-Boo". I started to say, "you know I'm sick." He gave me that look, and I said "Okie Dokie."

NO; FLOW

Only logic flow these lips.

Only pleasure between these hips.

Her juices flow sweet as the wine I sip. No longer sweet today he dipped.

What happened? He's the one that tripped.

I hate when your mouth flips.

You should have kept quiet, and your heart wouldn't be ripped.

In half.

Now you cry, you used to laugh.

Now you move slow, you were fast.

You feel like a failure, can't complete 1 task.

Can you do what is asked?

I know you're smart; but shut up sometime.

You have to Bury your pride to please mankind.

Wait awhile, then let your wisdom flow.

Hold your hips as tight as they will go.

Don't let them be pried apart until he can show,

that he's ready to give you more.

If not keep saying NO.

Let him propose to be there through all your woes.

Then marriage I suppose.

Now your lips can gratefully FLOW.

And your hips can pleasurably roll.

Issue

As a woman I think we get ahead of ourselves at times. Yes, we are beautiful, but we can be so seductive with our speech. Maybe because we know we have the prize. Sometimes we allow a man to get the trophy too soon and with little work. At first it seems like paradise; the wine is so sweet. Then were devastated when we figure out that he was playing us. He only wanted one thing. Then we begin to down ourselves and make excuses for why he left. I’ve learned to sit back and learn a little more. Then I will have more logic to flow these lips. I've decided that I will keep saying NO until he gives me a reason to let go and let my pleasure FLOW.

SUBMISSIVE BLUES

Yes! Yes!
I must confess.
I dress to impress.
I keep my head her dressed.
I strive to be the best.
Keeping ahead of the rest.
I'll take more than less.
I'm grateful I inherited her stubbornness.
I can wear my hair however I want to.
You can't tell me what to do.
Submissive to who?
Woman I know your hair ain't blue?
I submit this answer to you.
I have given you my body and my soul.
I will love you even when you're old.
All these years of tears that I've given you.
Does it matter that my hair is blue?
What I see as beauty you ridicule.
So do I submit an become seclude?
Should I dress down afraid that I will seduce?
What is it, that anything I want to do, causes you to argue?
I want to live too.

And who knows if I have many or few.

So, don't worry if my hair is blue. Help me to stop feeling blue.

Then I can be forever submissive to you

Issue

The Bible teaches us women to be submissive to our husbands. I think that some husbands abuse their power. Stressing about stupid things such as the length of your hair, the color of your lipstick, the size of your skirt, your career choice, and the color of your hair. I'm sure you all have many more to add to the list of SUBMISSIVE Blues. I don't care how happy you are, we all have our moments of downhome SUBMISSIVE Blues. To you men, stop being so forceful about these issues and make sure your wife feels like the beauty she deserves to be. I am pretty- sure that she will then love doing whatever you say, especially, when God leads the way.

YES

He said all the right things.

I've waited for this, so to him I'll cling

I'm so full of hope, knowing that if I truly strive

this thing called love, can forever thrive.

We will be partners in the fight for each other to survive.

We will vow to love. With this love we are alive.

I woke this morning and looked out the window.

How beautiful the world is when you're not consumed with sorrow.

I look back into your face.

Every inch of your outer and inner beauty, my eyes trace.

For the first time in my life, I have faith

they you plus I equal team winning the race.

He dropped to his knees. He cried please.

Lord blesses this woman to join me in holy matrimony.

Each day, I love I will keep confessing.

So, Lord, I ask for your blessing.

Yes I will wear your ring.

You said and done all the right things.

Issue

Will you know when it's right? Probably not, but God does. So, we have to pray that we are making the right choices when it comes to our mate. How many times has HE said all the right things and you fell deeply in love? It's happened to me many times but I'm not giving up. I believe that God has someone for me if I follow his lead. Maybe he'll be ordinary to you, but a beautiful sight to me. He may be poor of money but rich of love. I don't know just what he will be, but how happy I will be to finally say YES. I once had a friend that was like me waiting on the right man. One day she says she met this amazing guy in the store. She said that he was so respectful and charming. She thought about giving her number to him but when they walked outside, she seen him climbing in the passenger side of his car to get to the driver side. She said he nice, but she needs a man with two working car doors. I found this story to be so common but also so disturbing. Life has so many twists and turns. You can be driving a Benz one day and a pinto the next. You can be living in a townhouse then a dumpster. I think it's funny when people say they have high standards. Does that mean that they are high? There is only one that sits high and looks low. So, we are all low and will always feel the need to climb. So, you may get someone with more, but they're going to think they need to continue to climb also. Can y'all climb together? If you can, it doesn't matter what material things they have. Can his car make you say yes? Will you be there for richer or for poor? Yes. Will you be there for better or for worse? Yes. In sickness or in health? YES, YES, YES, That's the kind of love I want. When I can mean it from the bottom of my heart. He's going to say all the right things, but will we know that he really means it? Maybe not, but make sure you say YES to God, to yourself, and then to him.

I DON'T KNOW

Why do I torture myself?

With the reason or excuse that and why he left?

I didn't have a chance to beg "please don't go".

I became a statistic; The women that just don't know.

So, when they tell me, you're beautiful you're strong your're kind, I want to believe,

I just don't know, if so, why did he leave?

My soul is consumed with misery.

His unfaithfulness has blinded me.

Well, we took those vows there was no end that I could see.

I guess I should have kept looking and passed him up.

I was a food to believe that I have found my buck.

I just don't know, maybe it was bad luck.

Did I try winning in one night? I believed I rolled a 7/11.

A marriage made in heaven.

I don't know was I slapped back when I rolled craps?

Have I become a member of these mad black women, am I trapped?

I don't know can you tell me? Should I unleash this anger on you?

For all these years, I've held it in.

Can I move forward? if I don't put an end to where I've been?

I don't know if what you've done will affect all men.

I'm tired of hearing, there are some good men left.

I do know that God has the help me,

I can't do this by myself.

ISSUE

I always wanted to know why he left. I wasted years being bitter and angry at myself. I may never know why and I'm so thankful that I'm good with that. I turned to a man that will never leave me. So, ladies stop wearing about it. He is the one with the issue. He wasn't strong enough to deal with things. A chicken runs. So, uplift yourself. You stayed and took care of your kids alone. Momma's baby, Papa's maybe? They may decide to help sometimes. I'm tired of hearing that there are some good men left. I get so discouraged when I look at the shortage. But I'll say it again. I won't give up.

HEY NAPPY HEAD

Get on you little nappy headed thing

Did you know that you were affecting some of the most beautiful women in the world self-esteem?

Instead of focusing on their dreams, They're busy stressing over what you said with the image of beauty and blinded of what beauty means.

Being Excellent At Utilizing Taking You

Be excellent in whatever you do.

Excel at school, your job, your relationship, your diet, and combing your hair.

But do it for you.

Use what you got.

Utilize that walk.

Utilize that talk.

Use them lips.

Use them hips.

Use whatever it is that you like about you and everyone else will like it too.

I'm taking myself from you.

I'm letting my beauty come out.

To all the haters I shout.

I'm a beautiful little nappy headed thing.

and when I get in her chair and she tells me that my hair is all strings,

I'll get a new style that utilizes my eyes.

I have beautiful lips.

"I love your new cut."

I do too now watch me throw these hips.

You are beautiful, use what you got.

You can wear weave to your **** are natural dreadlocks.

Look at those eyes, that nose, them lips, them wide hips.

You are so talented you can do almost anything

nowadays you can rap if you Can't Sing

I'm proud to be a little nappy headed thing.

ISSUE

Hey nappy head hey I have found my inner beauty and is working on the outside of me. That's right inside out. Whatever you say to pull me down it won't work period I've learned to accept what God gave me to use and I'm working it. Haters get out of my way. You are a worker for the devil. Come on all the nappy heads in the world, let's beat him down. Satan's, your power is weak here period now listen up everybody, this poem is about releasing your inner beauty and working with what you were blessed with period that means that anyone can be a little nappy headed thing, so ladies be excellent at your works.

SALON QUEEN

You're not at the end of the road, you've just started to climb the Cliff

Don't slow down lady, keep moving swift

Will our last if I move so fast

You will never be in the past

We must tell your stories so everyone can share a laugh

No wonder why you got bad knees

Running through the store screaming I've lost my keys

I've been here for years but I can't figure out this computer thing

So are being on the keys now the darn thing wants to freeze

Somebody call a manager please

Nevertheless, you kept the salon going

Even through the years of doing D every Saturday morning

Is Patty coming yeah D she's never sick

I ran faster than her I'm tired of losing she's too damn quick

So yes D she's coming look there she is see her running

I'm late no Patty it's 750 we open at 8

I'll never forget how you refuse to quit always bright eyed and eager to learn

No matter how long you have worked here you understood a wrong turn

thanks for making this salon your main concern

You didn't have to clean while others said being mean like me

When you had no one on your book you smiled and got busy

Now look you're going down in history

The longest lasting beautician at JCPenney

You've taught us all a lesson

No matter how tough things get keep pressing its OK stop stressing

So, we're not going to let this day be depressing

Let's laugh and cheer Patty on

Her exciting new life has just begun

Now she can go have some fun in the sun

But will always be the queen of Carbondale JCPenney's hair salon

Issue

I am blessed to be a part of this wonderful woman's life. Patty Arbreiter worked at JCPenney salon for 32 years. She never slowed down until her knees gave out. I wonder if I'm going to have the same problem. Maybe I will, but it won't be from racing around the salon. I think I will take my time. I don't know about y'all but it feels good to be inspired. Watching Patty throughout the years, help me to believe that I can make it. Working with the public can be challenging. Sometimes you feel like burying your head never to return. She always returned with a smile and sparkling blue eyes so I can too.

INTERNAL LIGHT

Mirror mirror on the wall

Will I rise or will I fall

I look and you look back

Answer me am I on the right track

I have little left should I pack up and go

Are allow my stash to keep getting low

If you're doing right you will know

So who is that staring back at me

I am a image of who you used to be

No I'm looking at myself

Your magic mirror has left

Here borrow mine reveal yourself

Oh I see is death

Who is responsible for this that's not me

I've always been an image of beauty

This mirror that you've given me makes me look so thin

I've always wanted to be skinny but now I blow in the wind

Something has went wrong

And all skin and bone

My red hot hair was a beautiful sight

In this mirror my hair is all white

Who are you looking back at me

Don't you care what I look like

63

Mirror mirror where is the sunlight
Why is it this dark is this my final call
Answer me will I rise or will I fall
I opened my eyes
Wow did I rise
Mirror mirror what do you see
An image of beauty staring back at me
I can't make out the face but there's no misery
I see the sun there is no rain
Everyone looks the same
There's no moans or pain
There's no more night
I guess I've won the fight
Now staring back at me is a reflection of light

Issue

As humans, I think we get so caught up in our outer beauty, that we forget to make sure our most important part is in check. That is our inner beauty. All of a sudden, we look around and we're older and lost. Now how can we find ourselves? We're skinny, with no strength, our hair is white and dull. Well, there comes a time when this body will be irrelevant. So, our inner spirit must be ready to take over. God must be that inner spirit. Once he is, you will be able to look past flesh. Everyone will be beautiful in your sight. It could be raining but you will find the sun. Pain may be overwhelming, but you will find relief. Your night will seem bright, because you have fought so hard to win this fight. You found through layers of rough flesh your internal light. I hope you find it before your earthly body has gotten too weak. This light needs to shine so that people will believe that they too can find the light.

TESTIMONY

What do you see when you look at me

I hope you see a woman that let God put her in the lead

What do you see when you watch my smile

I hope you see a woman that's been running this race for a while

A woman that's ready to face any trial

So I ask her what do you see when you look at me

A woman that's always lively and so funny

But inspires me to be all I can be

So I asked him what do you see when you look at me

My future

Well what do you see in the future for me

Making you mine my wifey

I hope you see a woman that believes that prayer changes things

And he'll do for you what he's done for me

What do they when they look at me

I hope they see that through it all I am happy new line

Although they have done things to make me uneasy

I hope they see that I'm trying to be a better person and smile when I'm angry

I hope they see that y'all can't stop me

Why are you smiling I love my enemies

I used to hate but with the love of Jesus I've done a 360

Turning hate into love has set me free

Now what do you see when you look at me

I hope you see courage, strength, wisdom, beauty,

A woman who's ready to give her testimony

Issue

Unfortunately, we won't always know what others think of us. Some may find it uplifting to let you know the good that they see. Others may think that you may have the big head, so they might as well not tell you. Some can see nothing but negative things. I know people that tell the same stories about a person that was told 20 years ago. We can be so cruel how can a person ever redeem themselves if you are spreading old news. Anyway, I plan to love as much as I can and hope that I make a good impression on man so that I can inspire someone to wanna go with me to a peaceful land. So people every time you get a chance to testify about the goodness of the Lord, please do so. I want you to know what he's done for me. How he's made me and molded me into this woman who is proud to give her testimony. First giving honor to God, the pastor, members, and friends. I want to thank and praise the Lord for waking me up this morning and starting me on my way. He didn't have to give me this day. I'm thankful for the love that he placed in my heart. I ask you all to pray that I continue to grow stronger in the Lord.

ON THE OTHER SIDE

Can I do this can I let go

My dear friend, my love, I just don't know

My heart aches, so how do I get through this day

Maybe I will imagine what you would say

Girl it's OK. We will kick it again someday

We were close for a reason

So carry me in your heart until it's our season

Be there for our family and friends

OK cousin I will by keeping your memory alive

The memories of your friendship and love will help me survive

I love you and I will see you on the other side

Issue

This was a wakeup call. A young woman taking so quickly of cancer. No words can explain the pain that's felt. my advice is making sure you show someone and tell them how much you love them whenever you have a chance. I wrote this poem for a girlfriend of mine who lost a dear friend and cousin that was very young. My friend and I talked for hours about this devastating loss period the next week I had my first mammogram. I felt that everything would be OK besides, I'm young no cancer in the family and my breasts look and feel just fine. The letter stating that there was an abnormality came in a few days. At first, I felt weak, but began to pray. It turned out fine this time, but we never know. It is important that while we're here we be the best that we can be a best friend a best parent best kid best spouse the best coworker etcetera I want to see you on the other side

THESE HANDS

Thank you for my gift with them to the heavens I will lift

Praising that they were anointed

With them I will do what you appointed

At first I didn't understand so I wrestled with destiny

But I couldn't stop his plan

It was you that said use them wisely and they will be a specialty to man

Pray every day and negativity will not stand in your way

It will be present as it is in any place

Trust in me and I will prove your case

with this in mind I seen her cry

Because her hair was one-of-a-kind

So I pulled her coals they did unwind new line I lift her chin we met eye to eye

Why do you sigh

I don't like me she replied

I am thankful that in me she did confide

To bring out her beauty will give me great pride new line now she smiles and I feel joy inside

Again I lift them to the skies

Your blessings came down and my praises rise new line I admit when you chose me I was surprised

You call from heaven be a messenger of my plan

As you bring out of beauty with your unique gift

Them hands held by these hands

Issue

15 years ago, I was clueless of what I would do with my life. I had spent four years in college but didn't complete. I was 26 with two children and a husband in the penitentiary. I have always been a hard worker with lots of determination, so I became a legal hustler. I braided hair during the week and became an exotic dancer on the weekends. I wasn't proud of being a dancer but I was thankful to the Lord for giving me away to support to support my family. I continue to pray for a way that I could give up dancing. I had no clue that I would become a hairdresser. Yes, I braided hair but I hated it. Long hours for what, a couple of bucks. Sometimes I got paid and I owe you and never receive payment. Still, I was thankful for them couple of bucks. Finally, I started doing more than braids and someone asked, " have you been to school for this?" I responded with no; I never considered it. Then I began to think. What if I did go to school? They would have to pay me. I couldn't get grants because my student loans were in default. So, I decided to keep working as a dancer until I finished school. I had a plan to be the best beautician ever. That's just what I did. With daily prayer I finished school, got my license, and went to JCPenney salon eager to get a job. I was hired on the spot 13 years ago I've been the top stylist for 11 years look how God works over the years I have met some great people they have touched my life as well as I dares. I am overjoyed for my gift these wonderful hands God gave me. There have been so many times that I have been overwhelmed, not knowing which way to go. I have prayed Lord please don't let these hands fail me now. Each time, he has brought me out of difficult situations. I know that this beautician's hands are held by the hands of God.

DEAD ENDS

I hate when I go to a place that I've been over and over again
Get in a hurry and forget that this road leads to a dead end
I can't believe the situation that I keep putting myself in
Dead ends are becoming a trend
I bet if you have patience you could figure out
There has to be another route
There's a reason why they say
Good things come to those who wait
Leave early if you're always running late
Things will go and look a little smoother if you take some weight off your plate
A dead end may be the end if you continue at your rate
What is a dead end
A place where you go and go then you can't go no mo
As a beautician it's when your hair grow and grow then can,t grow no mo
I take out my scissors not to offend
But to rid you of those dead ends

Issue

I love the correlation of being lost going to a dead end and dead ends of hair. I have experienced trying to get somewhere in a hurry and being set back longer once I learned patience, I was able to solve my problem. I started leaving earlier to avoid travel situations. Also, I stopped taking on projects that I could never accomplish in one day period now I can breathe, I have a fresh start More than I have dead ends. My life and my hair look smoother without the dead ends. Just think how far you can go in life if you never reach a dead end. So slow down and rethink your strategy. It doesn't matter if it's somewhere you're going are a new hairstyle you will be satisfied if you wait for an outcome. I've had hundreds of clients over the years that have set in my chair and cried that they've been scaped. Sometimes I wonder if they would stop crying and listen to another round. If you want your hair longer then you need to sit back, take a deep breath and think about where you went wrong. Most of the time it's because you were impatient it takes too long to wash your hair once a week instead of once a month it cost too much to go to beautician, so you use the highlight kit. I know there are so many more, but it all comes down to the same thing patience. Stop stressing over simple things in life like the length of your hair and love yourself. You don't wanna end up dead.

I HAVE ISSUES

My eyes are heavy from looking at you

Yes I've had too much to drink I have an issue

No matter how hard I work to keep **** up

You constantly holler my life sucks

So you grown now get over my mess up

I don't claim to be perfect I just try to survive

As your mother I've always tried

Your needs I did provide

Food for you home for you the best is all I gave you

Now you say it's not enough

You're my biggest issue

My heart is heavy from loving you now that we're apart you told her that you don't like what I do.

When we were together you conveniently made sure that I had no clue

Now you ask why are you so angry Boo?

I have an issue

I remember the good times were great and the bad were few

When you decided to do you you acted like bad was all I could do

You broke your promise to who

When I vow to forever love you

Call me crazy if you want to

You are my biggest issue

My confidence gets low when I come around you

I love you because you are you

I've waited for years for you to say I love you too

So if you think I'm stuck in the past I have an issue

I was always respectful and obedient to you

You taught me the Bible and honoring you

Do the Bible say love her that I put in your womb or you will be doomed

I have loved you my entire life and this is true

I don't feel love back, so you are my biggest issue

Issue

Have you ever been told you have an issue? I have and most of the time is by those who I love most. I kept thinking if I have an issue then the biggest issue is loving you. Trying to please our loved ones can be so challenging at times period especially when they don't recognize what you go through for them. All the times you sacrifice so they could have a better life. I remember crying what's up to sleep many nights trying to figure out what to do or say. Now I have a revelation. I know I've prayed and it may not come when I want it but it will be on time period one day one sweet day, my love that I've given you will not be in vain.

I've grouped my issues in this poem by starting with the most hurtful ending to the lease so my eyes were heavy from looking at the image of me which is my girls. This issue causes me the most pain because I carried these girls in my body. I went through great pain to bring them into this world I could remember like yesterday when each of them was born. How I found the deepest love that I had ever known. So when they tell me throughout the years that I haven't done enough my heart aches. I know that I try so hard to be better than my mother was to me. I wanted my girls to have a gift that I didn't ever receive which was confidence talent and beauty. I have it somewhat now but when I was young I didn't. I cried out but no one listened. At times I feel that I succeeded in giving my daughters enough and at others I feel like a failure. I know I'm far from perfect but I would love for them to recognize me for some of the good that I've done for them one day.

My heart is heavy from loving my ex-husband. I recently got a divorce after being separated for four years period this man had me completely fooled. Instead of telling me what he didn't like about me he decided to disappear. Whenever I talked to him I asked but he still refused to say anything. He had no answer. Years later his mistress, told me all the things he didn't like about me. She actually eased some of my pain. I have been Downing myself for the wrong things. The so-called reasons for him to just disappear without even talking we're pretty minor. She should wonder what can she do wrong. Anyway, up until the day that he left he told me how much I meant to him. Yes, he really had me blind I'm still praying for my sight. It is coming back but still I have a long way to go. I know that this issue must be dealt with in my heart so that I can be a wonderful wife to my husband that God will send me.

My final biggest issue is my mother. This issue hurts but not as much as the previous two probably because I think what she done to me was not intentional. I don't think she understood how important it was to make sure that your little girl grew up with lots of confidence. How knowing that she is loved and beautiful can help her stand up against the world. I know she only wanted better from me but only pointing out negative things made my confidence so low whenever I go around her, I'm constantly making sure that everything about me and the person I'm with is perfect I hate that squinty look she gives when she is really displeased I often wondered how she could be a woman of God but find it hard to show love to her first born. Everyone around me tells me that I'm paranoid. I'm told to let it go and for the most part I have period the issue has helped me grow. I know that I can't live in the past, but I need to learn from it and move on. I also know that no matter what I disagree with my mother about, I will continue to love her and honor her forever.

I think I got it all out I hope these poetic words make you shout.

I hope they give you something to forever talk about

Some of you may disagree.

To a twisted poet like me it's a compliment. if it's worth me fussing, then it's worth discussing ,so here it goes, I have something to prove. I have nothing to lose as you've read, I refuse to hold in these issues.

Last issue

Have you ever wanted to say something to somebody but couldn't? will it a lot, but mostly about issues that won't step on anybody's toes. Sometimes I listen to others and I'm amazed that they can get away with speaking their minds and that I can't. I think that God made me to show them a kind person I have to prove what I can do with actions rather than with explanations. I know this because I often get hoarse talking to deaf people. Well they're not actually deaf but you would think so. I tried explaining myself clearly because I'm often taking the wrong way. Numerous times in my life people have told me that I said something that I didn't say because they only heard part of the story or refused to listen. Afraid that I may be redeemed. Redeemed is a very strong word it's what we should live to be. If you let me redeem myself from any situation, I may be able to start fresh every day. Maybe I will be overall better person. I want to be redeemed so I will start by allowing you to be redeemed I will not hold a grudge nor believe the hype I will find out the story by studying you all by myself if you say something that I don't like today I will let you redeem yourself tomorrow. When I started this book, I was so afraid to make one person mad I changed overall stories because I didn't want you to disagree. Then I realized that disagreements will cause conversations if someone disagrees with something I say in this book. I now take it as a compliment. If they are taking enough time to disagree with me then they are not deaf. someone may learn something from this person's reason for disagreeing period anyway comma who's to say that this twisted poet is always right. No one is except Jesus. So I can give my interpretation of a life issue however I please. Especially since this is my book and my issues this is easy I've never been able to say whatever I want to I have always written letters. Mama I'm sorry I disobeyed you please forgive me I love you. Yes I wrote it instead of saying it maybe it's because I wasn't brought up here in these words used very often. I have always been the first to say I'm sorry even if the other person was in the wrong. Somewhere along the way I became God fearing and I knew that hatred could not live inside of me. I had to release it and remember I'm not good with speaking to deaf people so I write it down hoping that they have sign so far I've only ran into blind and deaf people well they are blind and deaf when it comes to what I have to do or say I'm now waiting on my big day my stage will be so sweet I'll let anyone who's willing to work toward this goal get on my stage the goal is helping yourself as well as your neighbor get through the issues in life. Will people have sight when they read my book? Will they finally see Jerry for who she really is? Will they be able to read but not perceive? I hope they can understand. I don't want them to be blind death and inconceivable when it comes to me. Finally, I wrote it down so will you please listen to me?

Part 2

Deal

It is now New Year's Eve 2022, and I am going to complete this project that has been in the making for a decade now. These poems were written late 2012 and early 2013. I titled them "She snapped" and instead of the issue, I gave a Pow explanation of the reason for the poem.

Whenever, I decided to finish this poetry book, which was about a year ago, I came up with Will, Deal and Heal which would be the three categories. I look at these snappy poems as a time in my journey in which I started to deal with the woman that I had become and that would finish growing to be. Again, my purpose of writing these poetic thoughts down is to help someone else who finds themselves in a struggle to combat the things of this world that bring them down.

These poems seem to focus on male and female relationships. This is a time in my life when I wasn't married but was dating trying to get another husband. I would describe this time as feeling that I would always want to be a wife rather than just a girlfriend even if though my husband left me. These poems were also written after I was able to finally get a divorce. It took four years to get an address and money to pay for it. Before my divorce, I felt that I was double sinning with no way out. After the divorce, I figured at least the fornication could have a chance to stop after marriage.

SHE SNAPPED

DEEP IN SIN

He's inside of my skin

Now he's mad because I need to know what he's done and where he's been

If he stays away too long my skin is in danger of becoming too thin

I ask again where have you been

He said doesn't matter am I in your skin

Now I feel anger deep within

Has my body decided to side with sin

Has my skin gotten so thin

That he could see through me

Well can you see that my skin has cracked so I pulled back

When skin is so thin it hurts to be scratched

You stay gone too long

So I only know to do wrong

You stretch me then like a balloon I popped

My faithfulness and my courage dropped

Now my skin has become wrinkled and tough

You can't get in you're not strong enough

You wonder why I act like an old nag

You cause my skin to sag

Now she's on a leash that you drag

And she's pretty and perky you brag

Now you sided with sin and she's in your skin

Now it doesn't matter what she's done or where she's been

You are doomed because you will never B in another's skin

Pow

At the time of writing this poem, I was dating a man that was always doing something that I considered to be sneaky. One day he said that he was in my skin as to sarcastically say that I was all up under him. I wrote the poem knowing that he was not going to be my husband as he had no problem letting me believe that I was not beautiful, and that the young girl was. Well, I don't remember the entire story, but my thoughts stayed on a low insecure level most of the time anyway. I guess the moral is don't allow yourself to be so easily hurt by words. If your skin is so thin the ones who are close to you can make you pop like a balloon. Pow!!!!! Now you are sagging, and you look your age.

Flesh on flesh

Flesh on my flesh stress when I'm stressed

Yes this is a test

to be depressed

It's better but not my best

So you rest when I rest

Confess or be in distress

Have a little before you have less

Get some business before it's none of your business

Or I'll guess that you guessed

Flesh on my flesh

How can success evolve from a mess

How can you be blessed if you don't bless

my madness on top of your madness

Is a sandwich of unhappiness

so bless and be blessed

Before flesh is on flesh

Pow

Again, this is a poem written at the end of a relationship with a guy that I hoped could stay away from drugs. Well, all we had in common was a sex life that didn't get us anywhere. There was no happiness except when he fried chicken and potatoes for dinner. All I did was gain weight and hate myself. When I started to workout, he had a problem with my shorts being too short. I thought he really cared but it was just an excuse to fight me, and I became his excuse for staying out more. This poem was written because I had to be slapped in the face to realize that this relationship built on lust and the flesh was doomed.

Life is real

for goodness' sake

Stop being fake

It's easier being real

I won't break

Tell me the real deal

If for some reason you have the need to hate

Well let it out don't be fake

A tight-lipped smile may get you in your grave at an earlier date

Become genuine before it's too late

If you faker, then a $3 bill new line or then a placebo pill

It's time to be still until you can learn to be real

Life will never be a piece of cake

but can be sweeter when you stop being fake

So, for your sake

Even though it's your choice to make

At strongly advise that you realize there's no surprise where life leads when you're fake

POW

This would be realizing that someone doesn't want you. As matter of fact, they don't know what they want in life. This causes them to be fake in your presence instead of speaking the truth and facing the consequences. Most of the time this person who is trapped in their messed-up mind, will explode and cause harm to themselves or the other person. That's exactly what happened to me in this relationship. I ended up calling the sheriff and having this man removed from my house.

The voice

Boy does my life stink

I can't wait until I have that drink

A glass of wine will loosen me up every time

So if you're gonna stress me um the kind that you have to whine and die

You're stressing me so move now I can hardly sleep

I'm drinking a glass or two a day when it used to be once a week

The voice said that wine is not enough for the problems that you got

You need a good stiff shot

That wine will leave you where you at

If you wanna high get some vodka forget that moet

So I started taking shots before long I was drinking a whole cup

I'm more depressed than ever now my life really sucks

The voice said that alcohol is a depressant you are already depressed so that ain't what you need

I know somebody with some fire weed

Weed ain't no drug either it comes from the earth God put it here for us to smoke

When you're high you will laugh at any joke

Those nonsmokers didn't even laugh when the kid did that crazy stunt

They need to hit the blunt

Now life seems great I'm laughing and kicking it everyday

Year after year goes by then I realized that I'm stuck this way

Gotta sell dope so I can smoke

Can't get a job unless I passed the drug test

I've smoked up my profit

So how do I bail out when they make the arrest

My eyes are red and low my mouth is dry

For some reason I can't stay high

I need to get high before I die

The voice said Dang that weed is a hallucinogen make you feel like you're in a dream

Nothing is what it seems while you're high you dreamed life passed you by

Now you're so down every day feels like rain

I know let me introduce you to my buddy cocaine

You don't have to smoke it put it up your nose two to through a straw and where your mind goes no one knows

Now your eyes are wide open so can't you see

Everything that's happened in your life is where you thought you should be

You're on a new high so you listen to the voice instead of hearing me

The voice said don't listen to him you gotta do whatever to stay high

Cheat steal and always be prepared to lie

Anyway, you must stay high you can't come down you'll look like a clown

Do you know what you look like

Your clothes are dirty and raggedy new line if you're not high you'll look like a bum

Stay high so you don't feel dumb

Don't listen to him he's always right you don't want to receive your site

He will encourage you to fight

You're not strong you're weak you nobody keep listening to me.

POW

This was written as I was trying to make some sense out of drug addiction which continued to plague my small community. I unfortunately was a wine drinker and had begun to drink stronger drinks seeking a deeper buzz. Thankfully, I didn't graduate to the next level but was able to see how it could be easy to do so if you don't figure out why you need these substances. I began to think about it as a voice inside of us telling us that is alright, and we just need more and more to get us high and keep us there. The relationship had pretty much ended at this point as I found out that the man couldn't shake his drug addiction. This was his voice in his head, and I had no control over it. He was in denial. Anyway, the poem represents the everyday battle that we have with good and evil forces.

SECOND CHANCE

You're from around the way
I'm going to another town to find my bae
you seem nice and dressed slick
I heard the ones you've been with
some of them should have known to keep it zipped
I can't see myself getting with you
I know you can't be the one God gonna place me with
a piece of man is better than no man at all is a myth
anyway I know your Mama your daddy your whole family
too close for comfort and I stayed drama free
when we were in school you were not cool
you acted a fool didn't follow the rules
don't mean to sound cruel
how could I be with a guy like you
maybe if I didn't hear what you do still acting like a thug
pants sagging and the women got you bragging
and when it comes to church you still shrug
you be looking so thirsty
why do you have to be the first to do me
you may have been my first but you won't be my last
I'm going to the city and find me a man with more than cash
I refused to take on such a hard task

I will not stay here and put up with your ***

I have too much class

I'm going to find me a man that can take out the trash

slow down when he's moving too fast

love me although I sass

has bettered himself by learning from his past

and prays to God

let me and this woman forever last

Pow

This poem was written when I was again single but starting to turn more to God for guidance of the right man. I believed in second chances but was still confused that maybe this man could be a man of my past that changed to be one in the future. I was all over the place as you can read yet by writing these chaotic thoughts in poetry form, I began to deal with my issues of love and happiness ever coming to a desperate for love black woman. Eventually a woman like me would be healed. She would find a beautiful man that prays to God for her.

THE GOOD WIFE

How can you be a wife
when you refuse to change anything about your life
you're so full of rage you can cut him up with your eyes don't need a knife
you're strong willed but too weak to be a wife
if shutting up was your ultimate sacrifice
could you shut up even when he's wrong
nope he has to know that you're always right
so you argue and settle with the failure of becoming a wife
I like taking the inferior role
I came from his rib so he can run the show
that doesn't mean that I'm so low
the Bible teaches men to put their wives before their mother which is very high
he knows that for this marriage to survive
there must be a real woman by his side
beside every good man is a good woman
I need my man to be good
so it is very important in life
to become a Good Wife

POW

Here I am coaching myself into being a good wife one day. At this point I had failed, and I guess I was learning what may have caused my marriage to fail. I was willing to look within and correct what was wrong with me. This poem focuses on being humble and therefore stepping into the beautiful and important role of a Good Wife.

YOU CAN'T BLOW ME DOWN

First of all it took years to build this concrete wall

So if it is to come down you will have to be strong dedicated and in this for the long haul

If all you can do is blow smoke out your mouth

Those bricks won't budge

Use of hurt in pain will hold her grudge

She don't want to be alone

But refuses to deal with less right then wrong

So she becomes like a statue like stone

When the wind blows like paper you're gone

Now she's old her heart's like a mold

View with quick Crete

So one after the other she does mistreat

Dude get hard and go deep new line Yes she's hard as concrete

But beauty lies underneath

Her bricks are layered thick new line But she can be the one you want to get with

Takes a lot of heat to melt stone

So get your loving oh

Candy roses her favorite song new line is just what she needed all along

Now that you've became a man new line Toward these walls down

What's your plan

Can you take this concrete these bricks the stone and build an unbreakable home

One that will not bend from a strong wind

one that won't shake from the strongest earthquake

Ranked over the Richter scale

An unbreakable home chooses heaven over hell

These four walls were built from her hard wall

That you tore down by the power of love

When you choose guidance from the one above

So devil you can blow your smoke

I may even choke

But I won't allow my heart to be filled with stone

My walls are down but I am not alone

He stopped blowing smoke out his mouth

And love me until my bricks fell down

He took my dividing wall

and built a home full of love and on Jesus we call

So no devil can blow it down

POW

This is a powerful poem in which the woman begins to realize that she can never be loved as long as she keeps the hard stiff but invisible wall up which doesn't allow her to let anyone in to properly love her.

SHARE MY WORLD

This my music my beer my money my car and you are my girl

You are a major part of my world

Didn't you get my text I'll get home late and after I get some rest

I'll give you what I do best

Damn I overslept leave me alone girl can't you see I've been stressed

You know I'm trying to get my career off the ground

How can I rise if you keep putting me down

You know you love nice things so be patient have my back no matter how things seem new life right now my green has to buy me some green

That is the only way I can focus on my dream new line So if you are a part of my team then you will help me live my dream

Next page this **** getting old and so are you new line your hair done got Gray

your six pack is gone you sound like the rappers from back in the day

But I was by your side all alone new line all these years I fitted the bills

Confuse were you buying studio time are popping pills

I wonder was I ever a part of the world that you lived

Somewhere in your little brain you thought that one day you would give and your girl would forgive

Sitting on the couch with your oxygen tank listen about the news

Like you can stop the drought and still talking about your money in the bank you ain't got a clue

Of what's going on in this world

You didn't even realize that your girl stopped being a girl

and realized that she could never share your world

See I gotta be able to hang slang and bang if I'm going to make it through this thang

You are never happy always whining about the bills

I got you as soon as I get this record deal

anyway, you were paying bills before I got here

I thought we made things clear

I'll continue to stack racks

trust me I'll have your back

what you drinking tonight everybody knows your man pockets

swole keep a fat bankroll

POW

This poem was written out of frustration. While I was waiting on my good man, I happened to recognize the game that was taking place in many of the lives of our black women and men in society. It was like a game that always had an unhappy ending, jail, infidelity, diseases, kids with no father and more. In this poem I spoke on the feelings of both sides. The man felt like he was giving the girl what she wanted. She then says that the stuff had been going on for so long that the man didn't realize that he was old and grey headed. She said that she stopped sharing his world a long time ago.

CLOCKWISE

Imagine a huge rock on the other side was what you and everyone else always wanted

But had not

now there is really one-way around

you must walk in a perfect circle with both feet planted on the ground

This rock is so big that it could take a lifetime to complete this path

So you feel defeated after doing the math

Your mind begins to wonder can I go another way

If it's quicker I'll pay new line So you break the circle and go the opposite way

Causing some to fall they were in your way

Before then you weren't willing to pay

Who cares if they make it you trying to get what you were promised one day

So even though you keep knocking others back new line off the right track

Some even hit their heads on the rock

you ended their clock

you have no worries you're leading the pack

you look back

at the others going in the right direction

they are moving so slow

someone needs to tell them there is a quicker way to go

They've been walking for many years and haven't made it around the rock

I'm half their age and I'll be there in a couple of blocks

In passing I hear some of them talking about everlasting

That's exactly how long it will take at their pace

I would definitely win this race

By the time they make it I'll left them a couple of times new line I'm in a hurry to get mine

Since I'll be first I'll get the most

I may just take it all

by the time they make it most of them will have received that call

And those that followed me they're weak they will fall

So I made it where is the good new line there's nothing here I want I might as well stayed in the hood

So now here come the old people dancing around the rock

should I stop

these people crazy

all full of life

I'm feeling lazy

Well you rushed around the rock

much like you lived on the block

you chose the wrong direction

too impatient to seek perfection

so you're young and you made it around the Rock

You young but you ended your clock

POW

This poem had nothing to do with a relationship with any man. It was a spiritual awakening that I had and a development of a closer relationship with God. I started to understand that I must keep moving in the right direction and remain humble and patient. The goal of happiness was worth it. The journey around the rock was a lifetime of striving to do good.

DANCE WITH ME

I love church and I like the club too

Admitting to what you like says a lot about you

When I'm in church the spirit of the Lord lets me speak

His fire makes me move

When I'm in the club I sip on wine so I can groove

Music so loud I don't have to talk

So I concentrate on my high heel walk

Y'all go talking I know you used to cut a rug

Now you're perfect and you're the judge

There's nothing but devil in them clubs new line Shootings and killings and drug dealings

I love church I'm learning to put God first

But I'm stressed should I have worn this skirt

They shaking their heads like I'm dirt

Look at her in that tight skirt

Coming to church to make our men flirt

She's a Jezebel

She better get right she on her way to hell

There ya'll go nose in the air cause bad is all you smell

But it's you with the life that stinks

You claim the Lord but let the devil control what you think

You frown so stiff you can't even blink
Especially in the temple
God should be on your mind all the time
Then the power of God can save her even if she's showing her behind
I like the club I dress to impress
Some of them girls talking cause they look a mess
Scared his eyes fixated on this dress
I don't even want her man I want one for myself
And now he's not in here there's so few left
Now I'm feeling this wine
so it's about that time
I get in front of the mirror look at mine
And move to the music until my body unwinds
So y'all sitting stress while she's looking and feeling fine
Cursing to your girls she bet not dance by him he's mine
If you have such a jealous mind
Get off your **** and do something to better yourself so you can shine
don't wait until club over and grab her by
then your girls jump in her hair you know that ain't fair
So you bad now beat that girl like you wore the pants
She's still pretty and crying I just want to dance
I love God so back to church I go I look around and I see the eyes roll
Surely in the House of God they must believe I'm not a hoe
But it doesn't matter what they think they know

I must clear my mind cause it's praying time

When the mic is passed my way,

I'll have already prayed that I be used as a vessel today

If you don't want to love the spirit of God will make you love anyway

so if a skirt is tight let's praise him through the circumstance

Because all she wanted to do was dance

POW

This is a poem that was written when I started attending a church again in Cairo, Illinois. I have been through a divorce and was dating a guy that would never be a husband for me. I was connecting with God but felt anger of people looking down on me. I was confused. I didn't know what to do. I didn't know how to dress. I didn't know what the right way was to go. I was just wondering from church to church searching for something to help me live a better life. In this poem, I described the feeling of just wanting to dance which meant just wanting to enjoy life.

DISADVANTAGE OR ADVANTAGE

When you can't wear leggings to work

When cleavage shows in any shirt

You can't just get this way it's a family thing

When you're older to you he can still cling

When you walk past looks turn back real quick

Advantage or disadvantage of being thick

When you're on a diet you're toning

When she's on a diet she's boning

You don't need a push-up pull out trick

Advantage thick

When a flat chest in a low-cut dress symbolizes fit

But a big breast in a low-cut dress it's told to cover up

Symbolizes a ****

She's considered a model as her high heels click

You can't wear them your **** too big

Disadvantage thick

POW

I wrote this poem after getting tired of comparison of body types. I have always thought that all women are beautiful in their own way and that we all can improve our health and inner spirit which to me represents true beauty. I can say that the thick generation term can be a advantage or disadvantage when it comes to this world. Unfortunately, vanity is a big part of this world. it is what we base our likes and dislikes of people on, and your looks can get you a job quicker that being better at it. You have to prove that you better at it.

TREND SETTER

Just because I'm high profile
From the way that I walked to my unique hairstyles
Doesn't give you the right to put me in a negative spotlight
Using me as an example of things you do and don't like
If you're smaller than me you think you're too thin
if you're larger than me you think you fat exactly where am I at
I'm not the blame for your wrongs or rights
If you're put on the spot will you show some light
Frankly I'm tired of the fat that I can't do what you do
They like looking at me and close their eyes when they see you
you should see the eyes when I walk in
You would think I was a queen or something
They often say we never know what you're going to look like from day-to-day
Some of it seems genuine others seem fake
Envious because they are stuck that way
if they change anything someone may have something to say
Don't worry you don't have to bend
But don't hate me for setting the trend
I can wear or do something that hasn't been before
Some of you hate while others adore
And right before my eyes
my ideas have come alive

No longer mine or unique anymore
Now an abundance adores
Now they say I know why you look that way
You're trying to look like the girl on Tyler Perry play
Wait a minute when I wore that
Tyler Perry wasn't in
I was trying to set a trend
So because I'm in the spotlight
I can't go out at night
If I do someone would tell
and I don't want you blaming me for going to hell
So look deeper feel me
Just because I'm trendy
there's more beneath this surface that you see

POW

I wrote this poem one day after dealing with a typical day at the styling salon. I was constantly criticized for being me which was different than all the others. I didn't stress about beauty or looking for a new look, I created beauty that my eyes could vision. It seemed that it was hard for me to fit in with most of the other women that I worked with except when they wanted to try something outside of the box. Isn't that ironic, they came to the one that they left outside of the box for solutions. I wasn't boasting with this poem, but I had to vent so I did in poetic form.

WHERE IS LOVE

Looking for love but never getting it
Try being the original unique me but you weren’t feeling it
So I change done things I've never before
Justify another closed door
What the hell my heart can't take this **** anymore
Everything I do is wrong
Gave you money even wrote you a love song
In between the sheets I only hear my moans
And my question is is it good or it's your love that I long
What is wrong with me every day I plead
I'm always in need
Is this necessity or agree
Maybe he's given all he can and it's enough
Maybe I'm a strong woman that's too tough
And enough just ain't enough
Should I choke on my words and hide how I feel
Should I be fake or accept what is real
I asked for guidance at night when I kneel
So why should this decision be such a big deal
I asked you to speak for me but question if I spoke right
Lack of fate would torment my soul night after night
It's painful to know that my feelings caused the fight

Is there a happy ending insight
I know things come to those who wait
Well I'm tired of waiting
Sick of dating
Body too old to keep mating
and I'm sick of worrying about my one through 10 rating
Getting old
still turning heads
So I must be at least an 8
Lost a couple letting you decide my fate
When it love so bad I was willing to take
Now I have a congenital heartbreak
I didn't find love and now it's too late

POW

Here I go back on the relationship roller coaster. At this time, I have decided to date again and I am confused about where things are going. I have never been one who wanted to just date around and mess with different men so after feeling like he was the one and upping the goods when I should have not, I felt insecurities all over again. I began to question Where is Love? I was tired of looking and to impatient to wait.

SISTA

My beautiful women don't get frustrated

You must realize that the unfortunate way of the world has his brain sedated

He knows not himself

he didn't think before he left

he couldn't help but to want her who is highly overrated

As a real sister I hate it

If we get a little big we're fat

If we get a little skinny then we smoking crack

If she's a little big too they say she the new kind of thick

If she's skinny then she's a model chick

So my sister you got the right to be mad

And know this before he die he gone wish he had

A beautiful God-fearing big mouth big **** nappy head

and whatever we have been labeled

Real sista by his side

POW

Woo! I was really getting frustrated myself and trying to convince myself to calm down and forgive these foolish black men for leaving their sista's . I was tired of seeing my family and friends alone with no man to help them raise their kids. Everyone of the black men in Tamms, Mounds, Ullin and of course Cape Girardeau were infatuated with white women. The Sista's started wearing blonde weave and more. They looked and seemed desperate but at least they got attention even if they didn't get a husband just more kids.

MOTHER

Maternity is forever green and planted like a tree
Ovulation to creation was by God
So I can't spare the rod
Taken from the rib of man
then after several weeks of excruciating pain
You were taken from me
half of me his half traveled
then you rode my body with no saddle
Eternity whether you live it or not
A mother is to be forever so grateful for who you got
She the Reason that you and I are here today
First give honor to God then the woman that he allowed to give you a birthday
mother's such a powerful gender
The description of a woman that has become more than herself
she is always living for her child
so she is maternally green and planted
like a tree with God in control
she is strong, grounded
held by her roots and unmovable

POW

This was a poem I wrote for Mother's Day that summed up why we should always respect the woman that birth us. We damaged her beautiful skin, and she loved us more than anyone in the world.

SHIT GOT REAL

Is this how he felt
when I was too depressed to give him what he needed
did he feel stupid as he pleaded to someone else
listen to his goals and how his day was
if he felt good or not
did she make him feel that he was on top
when he said hey honey and I just said hi
did he feel like going away to cry
when he gave his all to support us and our bills
was he saddened as we made fun of him still
all I can say is I'm sorry I know how you feel
maybe this poem will help me heal
I put you through so much drama
I hate the ***** named karma
I remember pushing your hands away
now I wonder what I should have done to get you to stay
I couldn't forgive you of your trespasses
I decided to punish you as if I was your master
felt like I created you
and who were you to think that you could do what you wanted
that's not the picture that I drew
is this how he felt

this is how I feel

when it happened to me

shit got real

Pow

This is a banger. I was going through a tough phase of self-analysis. I was dealing with a demon inside of me that would have to be destroyed if I was going to ever have some peace. I could not walk around another day wondering why my husband Shawn left me. I had to deal with it and accept responsibility. It was my fault. I didn't have room for forgiveness because I was full of anger, hate and rage. I was God fearing enough not to kill him but not enough to stop the internal hatred going on in my soul that was killing me. All I can say is this is the real deal. I'm hoping that I can help another sister get to the next step which is to Heal.

The Hairs on My chin

Deep in the about what's happening now and way back then

as I pull the hairs out of my chin

I can't believe what goes on now

people help your kids curse their mama's out

back then you were smacked

if you act like you wanna talk back

disobedience is a scary sin

when you live to pull the hairs from your chin

here and now

everyone has to be rich to have a wanted baby or make a vow

back then people fed them kids the best way they knew how

back then people were more grateful so showed respect

now all you can give is what they expect

so you keep on giving and all you want is a grin

instead they frown as you pulled the hairs from your chin

will they ever know where you've been

do they remember how shapely you were before you became thin

would they love and respect who you were back then

when you had a good job nice car and plenty of money to spend

when you die

will they pull the hairs from your chin

115

POW

This was written as I was feuding with my girls. They seemed to be so insensitive and feel that every penny that I made should go to their selfish desires. They were always pointing out my wrongs and rarely felt that I did any good for them. So one day as I noticed the hairs on my chin and remembered plucking grandma's chin, I wondered if when I die, they would make me presentable and get them ugly whiskers off my chin.

NOT ME

I used to think
that I needed to find the missing link
for years I dealt with his promiscuous behavior
I loved him so twice I bared labor
I couldn't stop searching for what was missing
felt like an infinite puzzle that I'm fixing
there has to be an answer you have me why do you need her
what is this connection
you have made me dislike my reflection
I move forward yet you go in the opposite direction
I know you love the children but I'm certain you don't love me
I used to feel that my love for them kept me from leaving
now I know you inhale the love like the air you breathe
so you do enough to make sure we don't leave
knowing that my heart can't watch them grieve
suddenly I realize that she is ugly
to not think about them in misery
and I made peace with the truth
it's not me

POW

This was written after a conversation with a lady that I knew who was going through life feeling this way. This caused her to do things that wasn't right. All I could do was write. I tried to console her with the poetry, and it seemed to work. At least she could begin to deal with the situation and heal for her children. It is so important to seek within and heal so that the future can have a future.

THE BLOCK

Don't want no nigga off the block
If his eyes big that mean he smoking rocks
If his eyes low that weed got him blowed
Most of the time you can tell who broke
Is it mid, loud, or home grown they smoke
Doesn't matter, I don't want no nigga on the block
Most likely he not gone put a rock
On my finger
He wants to be a rapper instead of a r&b singer
He may have to think
Back to the day
When he heard the preacher preach and the mothers pray
Father don't let my son grow up and stay
On the block all his days
I remember her prayer
I was also a church member there
Praying why the niggas on the block don't care
I want a man that go to church with me
One who fears God enough to get on his knees
Instead of wanting drugs
I want him to crave me.

Love me around the clock

Work hard and have nothing but time to speak to the niggas on the block

POW

This was written as I rode past my ex-boyfriend that I knew couldn't be a husband. I spoke on him in earlier poems when I was dealing with letting him go. This would be my confirmation as I saw him on the block doing his usual. I watched so many men lose their homes, wives and children because they loved the block more. Or shall I say the rock more. I was determined to wait on God and get the husband that I deserved.

WATCH YOUR WEIGHT

Watch your own weight stop watching mine
Rather I'm on the incline, the same or on the decline
Don't worry about mine
I'm still fine
Stopping her from eating bread
All because you don't like how your hips spread
Some will have hips no matter what they have been fed
So watch your weight
Stop watching mine
If you look so good
Why do you worry how I should
You are wasting your time
I don't care about your straight line
If you think you straight
Get a mirror and watch your own weight

Pow

Sometimes you feel like snapping out on people who study your body every time you come around. It's so obvious that they are looking at you and can't wait to say something about your appearance. Most don't look as if they care about their own.

OBSESSED OR POSSESSED

Is this obsession or just an expression?
Feeling crazy for always giving a confession
I confessed to the crime when I didn't do it
I confessed my love hoping they knew it
My heart is explosive so with one wrong move
They blew it
This life blows me
Why do I feel so deeply
As my mind spirals
And the night keeps me
My flesh is shallow, and you easily hurt me
Yes I am complexed
My feelings must be carefully expressed
So that they won't think I have given less
Now if you guess
Do you often pass the test
Can you guess your way through life
Better yet can you guess
That you are ahead of the rest
Am I obsessed or possessed?

122

POW

OBSESSED: to preoccupy or fill the mind of someone continually, intrusively and to a troubling extent. Constantly worrying about something.

POSSESSED: completely controlled by an evil spirit

Wow, which one of these definitions best support this poem. I wrote it dealing with relationships and why they didn't seem to work for me. Was it that I needed to free myself of evil spirits?

CHANGE OF LIFE

Don't need no fire don't turn up the heat
I have something burning inside of me
I stand all day come home and you take away my seat
didn't eat no salty meat
yet I still have swollen feet
mad because I continue to teach
that the goal is never out of reach
stop nagging over and over you preach
I can't help it you see
inside of me a little before a little after 40
my body started yelling lordy lordy
what's happened to me
were there used to be a tingle
has become replaced with a wrinkle
where there used to be laughter i
t's now replaced with failing my happily ever after
sometimes I consider becoming a nun
locked away with women of my age who have something in common
I don't like these that live here
they make me feel that the end is near
when they're cold I am hot
plus they seem to take all that I got

whatever I do is never enough
they say that at this age I should be the stuff
I should be and have more than they ever had
Be held to high standards
so those behind me won't be mad
now how am I supposed to last
when at this age I'm still held accountable for my past
how do I go on
when they treat you like a stranger in your own home
never mind the fact that most of the time she is paying the loan
by this time in life the man has already left
robbing you of your pride, confidence and faith
he should be charged with Grand Theft
He can stay away
until he can be what's expected of us today
the work in the church is even done mostly by us
at this age it gets harder to listen to the preachers fuss
especially when we're living a life that we hate
we're tired of going on dates
Pissed that to get pleasure we have to fornicate
so we pray for our sins again and again
feel like giving up but we can't because there's something burning within
at this age our body goes through hot flashes it could be 20 below and we still managed to sweat
yet we still work ourselves to death because we are expected to be perfect

how do we go on

then there was the mother's song

it feels like fire shut up in my bones I

'm in love with a man who would never do me wrong

the joy that he brings me allows me to want to go on

and see what the end gonna be

young lady you haven't seen strife

get on your knees and thank him for the changes of life

POW

If you've never been through nothing then you can't be brought out. this poem was to help you realize what to shout about. now when you've really been changed, you will know why the old folks want afraid to die and why everybody don't sound the same when they sing. I know I've been changed the angels in heaven sign my name. now ask yourself what can you do to help someone who is going through the change physically spiritually or both. if you are going through the change what can you do to not burn the ones around you or should I say freeze those close to you? since I'm going through both I'll start with saying if you know that your loved one is always hot then offer to turn down the heat. I'm not talking about the thermostat I'm talking about the tension between you. this tension is caused from them refusing to step up and take the load off the changing person. I don't know about you others that have hot flashes but being able to kick back and relax more feels good; just as good as an air conditioner. so look turn down the heat and compromise when you know somebody is hot. make the temperature comfortable. this helps physical and spiritual change. if I don't be pushed into cursing you out, I would feel closer to God and therefore receive more growth. I hate when love ones refuse to go to church then remind you every time that you do wrong, you're just a hypocrite. You don't go to church how come you cursing at me? stop causing the heat to rise. if you know it's getting hot in the room, give us some space. now what can we do to help those around us cope with our transitions? as far as the hot flashes, instead of turning the heat off leave it on 68. put a fan on your side of the bed. dress like when travelling so that windows can stay up during the winter. As for the spiritual change, about all you can do is pray. see the devil don't want this change to occur, so he loads us up with anybody and everybody's that he can use to take your faith away. so pray pray pray and fight off the devil. be aware that the devil will cause those you love to speak and do things that they don't want to do. by knowing these acts are of the devil , we can become one step ahead. so trusting in God helps us turn down the heat by putting the devil's flames out.

PART 3

HEAL

Well, it is January 11, 2023, and this journey has become easier. These poems go back to 2014 to the present. As I read my earlier work, I understand that I still have a long way to go but that something clicked in my soul that would allow me to open my heart and receive knowledge that would allow me to grow into the woman that is writing her heart out to you today. I am a woman who has walked into my purpose of life. Yes, I feel better from the Balm that has been rubbed all over my physical, mental and spiritual being.

I have not named the title of these poems because the name would change by 2023 and therefore, I would have to divide this section in which I just don't want to do. I know let's call it SHE HEALS. This would be appropriate as you can see a pattern. I am a woman who with her testimonies of healing can help others to heal.

By the end of this section, I will transform my writing into present time. I will write poetry as I feel in this moment. This beautiful healing time of my life. I have a lot to say a lot of sermons that I have written. Why not share some of them in poetic form.

The explanation of these poems will be called Balm.

It took years for me to understand a song that was sung in churches. Is there a Balm in Gilead? I thought it meant a Bomb and that's what I sung. Recently, a Minister of the Nation of Islam explained the healing Balm to me.

SHE HEALS

PEACE

I woke this morning feeling down

Then I realized that I was cursing God, so I opened my eyes and looked around

There is no devastation today in my town

I looked at the smiling baby and she will erase any frown

So, as I wait on my day

That I will awake and not feel the same way

I must be thankful that I woke in a town

With a peaceful sound.

BALM

Sometimes, we can be so selfish. All we think about is our own emotions. This will cause us to wake up in the morning and not give thanks to the one who didn't allow us to die in our sleep. We are also selfish to not pray for those in our neighboring towns who are going through so many trials. We can be safe and still find something to complain about. Well, this poem was written as I was being selfish. I was probably sad that I didn't have a man or didn't have a husband. Probably sad that I never seemed to have enough money or have a perfect look. I would then look over at my grandbaby who was around two months old and notice that she was grinning. Lyla is her name and today she is eight years old. She will be 9 in April this year. Her smile brings me peace. She is a balm for painful hard-hearted people. Let your hearts stay open and full of love and I guarantee you will get some healing.

LISTEN UP

If you dark skin
Don't be trying to get around other dark folks
And act like light skin folks ain't shit
Light skin folks stop acting like the sun only shine on you
Skinny girls stop rolling your eyes when a big girl eats cake
If you think you so cute, who cares if she big
Big girls stop calling every other big girl cute
"She got a pretty face" size don't matter
Big butt girls stop acting like you the bomb because of your butt
And acting like her butt flat cause it ain't dragging behind her
Flat booty girls stop saying at least my lips big and face pretty
Dudes with a little money stop acting like broke dudes don't deserve happiness
Broke dudes stop wining about "you want him for his money"
Get off drugs
Church folks stop judging those who do things you used to do
Remember where you came from
Sinners stop calling church folk hypocrite
Just because you don't want to do right
Everybody stop making sin and other things suit your situation
Stop making your Heaven their Hell.

BALM

Woo, this was written as a thought that would promote my stage play that was based on my novel, in I'd Rather go to hell than the Heaven that you're in. The play was titled Is My Heaven Your Hell? Basically, if we loved ourselves, then we wouldn't use the things about us, to put someone else down. Instead, we would promote peace, joy, and happiness to everyone who came around us. When you understand that we all have a mountain to climb, you stop being so high. When you are humble, you can be healed and promote healing through the way that you live your life.

MORE

Again and again, I'm tired of being crushed

I was too naïve

Guess I look like the floor to you

Guess this is the door for you

I'm sad but being your fool

I won't do

I refuse to put up with any more excuses

Of how sex is right

But marriage is useless

Who needs to sign a piece of paper

Only to ignore and break the contract later

You rather live in sin and gamble with your maker

Well do us women who want more a huge favor

Pretend she drowned and you just couldn't save her

Let us be dead to you until you are reincarnated

Because this life full of strife

As we strive to be your wife

Ain't that damn complicated.

BALM

When you realize that you deserve more, is when you desire more. You will then attract who and what is right for you. A life that is soothing.

WINNING

My world is upside down and my head is spinning
I need to be praying but I find myself sinning
Happiness doesn't last long if the devil is winning.
Now I'm headed once again to failure and his red ass is grinning.
He laughs while convincing me that if I want to feel good, I must be sinning
And winning
He makes me too hot
I need to cool off fast, but body goes into shock
So I died but not
Before I answered rather, I wanted true happiness or not
I chose for my head to stop spinning
My mind was not submitted to sinning
And by choosing happiness
I died and went to heaven
Look who's winning

BALM

We all must die or destroy the old self to become new. If we want Heaven, we have to destroy the environment of hell that we created within ourselves.

ONE OF A KIND

I've worn braces to straighten my teeth/ now do you love me?

I've done squats to get this booty/ do you love me

I've brightened my dark spots with bleach/ do you love me

I've changed the way that I speak/ do you love me

My hair is perfectly weaved/ do you love me

I've gotten a mater's degree/ do you love me

Now there's noting wrong with these things/ but when you are trapped in the learned behavior of the worlds view of vanity

Your will never be internally pleased

You will be filled

Still

With depression and insecurities

Stopping you from living

Sinve you have been taught these things from generation to generation

The cycle has to stop turning completely around and move in the opposite direction

Instead of spending hours looking at your physical reflection

Spend some time learning how yu look on the inside

By studying the mirror of your mind

Find your spiritual connection

When you begin to rise, all bad will be at your feet

Including the misrepresentation of beauty

Your thoughts control what you can be

So ask yourself is that important to me

What is that going to do to help me

Hopefully you will choose to climb

Out of this worldly prison the mind

And be one of a kind.

BALM

When you let go of the mental programming of the mind that has been instituted by this world of Satan, you will be able to live each moment in freedom. Just try to imagine that you are the image of a beautiful god. You were created to show the world how beauty looks, talks, thinks, loves and lives. Just by being you. Now, I know that because of circumstances, our teeth may get overly spaced and so forth, but you can't let that be what determines how you feel about yourself. If so, you will never have happiness while you are here in this world. basically, if you are trapped in the cycle of beauty secrets, you will not be living. Your mind is too focused on outward appearances, to enjoy the beauty all around you. You will miss out on so much, if you don't stop being consumed with Satan's world's view of beauty.

SO I WRITE

Sometimes it's difficult to cope with thee many challenges of life

So I write

If I speak my mind, there may be a fight

So I write

Plus my voice is stern no time for mess

I rarely lie and if I do, my tongue is quick to confess

I'm always trying to make it right

But rarely understood

So I write

I feel like I'm ging crazy can't sleep yet I dreamt all night

My screws aren't tight

No one to talk to

So I write

Everything around me is dark so I pray for some more light

And I know that I have the light

But sometimes I lose sight

I need more guidance

Why do I cry

All I do is try

But I'm rejected

So I write

BALM

What a way to heal which is by writing the way that you feel. Keeping your mouth closed can go a long way throughout your healing journey.

I HAVE A QUESTION

Are you really concerned if others go to Heaven? I'm confused

Why are you trying to point out that someone doing something that you don't do

I have yet to see such a person on this earth who does no wrong

Are you really trying to lead them to heaven or help them surrender to hell

Sone of ya'll on the book calling others in church a Jezebel

I've went to church all my life

And all my life I've had to fight

Not with my fists, but with my mind

You see I had to shut up and not speak, it wasn't my time

Yet others gossiped saying whe asked for prayer cause she drank too much wine

So I'm confused

I know I'm a sinner How about you

I believe that God loves everybody

How about you

I love going to church but I am confused

I have enough stress on my job and everyday life

My church should me a refuge

I'm confused church folk

I have a question for you

Do you expect others to look and act just like you

You did this that way so they better too

You dress so pretty that dress hang just right

So is hers too tight

I have one more question for you

You rather run off those who don't do what ya'll say do

I guess there is only a holy few

My answer to you is this I've been holding my tongue afraid of being disrespectful and called wrong

But maybe someone must tell the truth

Keep living in that circle that doesn't allow those who

Ya'll determines aren't good enough to come through

And maybe they will decide that if you going to heaven

That they don't want to be in the same heaven as you

BALM

Holier than thou is the phrase that a lot of us on this journey are labeled and it's because we become just that. We must stop and remember where we came from. If our mission is to help others live a life in the garden. Heck, if we want to be in the garden, then we must humble ourselves, study more and pray that we can live a life that is pleasing to God and therefore be a walking example for others.

BY MYSELF

If there are no good men left, I will stay by myself
If all you have to offer is physically felt
I'll stay by myself
I'll stay by myself
Was apart before death
To death do us part
Who knows what that means
That we stay through all the beatings and infidelity
Now how many of us would still have him if we accepted these things
"gurl you was with him last night, but I wear his ring"
Yea I want a ring but can't accept some things
So I will accept the name calling from a hoe to being crazy
You crazy wow now ask yourself what does that mean
Crazy because I rather have a king
Crazy because with or without one I've always done my thing
Crazy because I am willing to wait for the one who waited for his queen
The one that although life gets hard, makes me chase my dreams
Dreams what do they mean
Something that you think of awake or asleep that's not yet happening
Let's make it happen hand in hand step by step
If you are going come on or I'll go by myself

BALM

Have you ever had a conversation with a group of women about men that blew your mind? Well, that is exactly what happened to me. I saved the ending to represent the woman that I was trying to become. The one with the big dream. I'm not trying to put the other women down, because I have kind of been there but not quite. I just could never get into the married men thing but to each her own. We all have to learn and some harder than others. Most of these women who have been satisfied with being the other woman are really shattered and need help. My dear Black man and my dear Black women we have to rise out of this lower self and rise into our dreams or what life should be.

I CRY

Days like this I cry as I look out at the gloomy gray sky
And begin to wonder why
My true partners in life had to fly
Away and leave me crying
Reminiscing of days of old
As I look down the road
I can still smell them and hear the stories they told
Some were funny some were sad
Some made you mad
And some were scary
Like the ones about looking in the mirror at Mary Mary
Sweet Contrary
But oh how I would love to hear their voices once again
The voices of wisdom and strength that didn't allow their families to give in
So I keep walking down the road and hoping to sniff and smell
The white beans greens and even the stinky chitterlings
Being cleaned
But there's no one doing these things
They busy trying to have material things
Which are ok but we get lost
And no longer care about the cost

The cost of losing all the memories

Who remembers Mr. Leroy, Bob Woods, Charlie Robinson, Mr. Foots, Mr. Fletcher, Mr. Daniel and JC Price

These were real men

Who took care of their kin

Who remembers taking the slop to the pig pen

Yea it stunk but I wish I could smell it again

Now I know why I'm single as I cry

For one of these type of men

Days like this I cry and wish there were houses here instead of grass

But material vanishes only memories last

BALM

When I wrote this piece, I had dreamed that the man that would be like these men would come into my life. I posted this poem on Facebook and that man who is my husband today, commented " that is really good. Sounds like something Toni Morrison would write." I had never heard of her, but I was so thankful that he paid attention. I had been wrestling with feeling of loneliness and wishing that those who had died were still alive. Never forgetting but moving on to the future helped me heal. So cherish the past, admire the present and live for the future.

SHE IS AN ANGEL

She is an Angel

She was placed in our lives

For a short period of time

But touched every heart with her glassy doll eyes

She blessed this earth

And no matter the hurt

It was for a limited amount of days

However, she left a story for everyone to say

She had healing in her smiles

Joy in her laughter

She was always ready for her pictures to be captured

Thank God for the memories that we can all share

We will miss theis Angel but she's in his care

I know that these words will not erase pain

But one day you will accept why another Angel has been gained

Fly baby fly keep on smiling

From heaven smile down on me

Sweet Angel Baby

Keep on smiling

BALM

I'm sure you can tell that this was written after the death of a baby. It tore my heart to pieces to listen to my little cousin ask me where her baby is at as she lay in a hospital bed not knowing if she could walk again. I missed her baby but her baby couldn't come back and all we had was her. We had to hold it together so that she could get strong enough to come home. I wrote this for myself and then decided to give it to the family. I didn't care if they read it at the funeral or put it on the obituary, I just wanted it to be there for us all in the future. Well, my little cousin has another beautiful baby girl. She can't replace Chloe, but she replaced the pain with joy.

YOU YOU YOU

You may not have a big butt
You may but also a girdled gut
You may not be thin
You may but blow in the wind
You may not be toned
You may be toned to the bone
You may not have large breasts
You may but they hand down off your chest
You may not have smooth skin
You may but it was wrinkles waiting
You may not be light skinish
You may but see every blemish
You may not be the new in dark skin
You may but your chocolate is melting

BALM

There's no need to point out the flaws of others trying to make yourself look and feel better. Be You and hold your head up. Smile at everyone don't frown. We are all different. Being you don't have to mean putting the opposite of you down. When you learn who you are, your you can go far without trampling down on someone else.

WHITE WOMEN WINNING

This guy once told me that “black women don’t jog
They don’t slob
They have to wear weave for their drains to get clogged
I replied
Well when we jog, we can’t wear shorts
Because the minds of men become distort ed
Some just give up and yes that’s retarded
But what’s worse is that we are constantly downed
If we don’t speak proper like her, then we are being profound
The fact tht she can jog in shorts that are much shorter and no one care
Not the church folks or other men they marry her
Oh I know it’s because you like our natural beauty
We can hafe a nappy head no lashes but better have a big booty
We are held to such high standards and if we excel then were snooty
If we ask you to help out then you left cause she was moody
Yea I may be since there are things I won’t deal with
There is an advantage to being beautiful, smart and thick
I can pull another real quick
But this poem is not to down you.
It’s to express a feeling.
Black church women I love you I am one too.

Black men be our men.

But both stop just because our shorts are short don't mean we're sinning.

While you're downing us, they winning.

Look at Hilary Clinton

If we don't look like Michelle, then we're not crap.

You showing too much ass you need to get slapped

However she show her bones and she's in the swimsuit edition

Can't you see we are crying and using whatever to get you to listen we need attention

Now this is not just about me and my feelings.

There are many who need defending.

So, come on black divas let's step our game up

This conversation with dude was deep.

I tossed and turned as these thoughts bothered my sleep.

Everything she do if we do the same we are judged and are the only one that is sinning

We must pray because we are all the reason why white women are winning.

BALM

This poem was written after I first ran into who would now be my Mother and law at the grocery store. I had just finished working out and was trying to hurry to buy dinner and cook for children. I was a single lonely black woman that although I really was trying to lose weight, was also hoping to turn a few heads. By being judged because my clothes were inappropriate, I didn't feel very good about myself. I enjoyed the compliment from the man in the store also who ended up finding a way to date me. I knew deep down that something wasn't right. Lust is all it was and that could never be the basis of a relationship. Well, he wasn't looking for a relationship. He was looking for some thick black woman like myself to lay up with. I am so thankful that my Mother and law who didn't have any idea that she would become that, was bold enough to make me feel ashamed and realize that I needed to put on some clothes.

The second thing that sparked this poem was a conversation with a black guy that dates white women. He basically said that black women weren't as nasty in the bedroom as black women and that we weren't as pretty without weave in our hair. I was furious with him but because of self-hatred, I felt this way about my own self. I wouldn't get caught dead without my weave and eyelashes. I would be jogging, and the eyelash glue would be burning my eyes. I would keep pinching them and making sure that they didn't fall off.

Anyway, we must all fall in love with ourselves so that we can stop losing. You can't have real love when you are not the real you.

KISSED

You chose the wrong woman now you live with regret
So you try to ridicule me wishing we never met
Every time I walk by she was by your side
But the corner of your eye caught my every glide
While you lusted, did you remember the times
You brought tears to my eyes
I laid there many nights
Without hope for love but hoping that after the fight
I would conquer the strife
And remain in this life
Can I sacrifice
A moment of pleasure in exchange for a better life
At times you had me thinking that I was your wife
Just couldn't understand how you could be so trifling
You could care less about committing a sin
So now look at you and her
She fat but her personality good
She loud but she does things you never would
Well it's like this I'm from the hood
Can't stop thinking about the fact that your momma said
My boy ain't no good
If you haven't left him yet, then you should
His favorite number is 6

He wants nothing but a quick fix

Even at your expense

So now except that you've finally been kissed

If I'm nothing, subtract me from your list

BALM

This is all about accepting what could never be and understanding that it's ok to not be for someone who is entangled in a messed-up life. This man in this poem only loved drugs. The woman in his life, had to compliment his lifestyle in some kind of way. In the end, he regrets his life and realizes that he was kissed by someone, a woman who deserved more. This woman would feel like she was nothing. Healing took place when she removed herself from his list of women to be used.

FEAR & INSECURE

Plagued with insecurities

Causing me to do whatever he asks of me

If he says jump up and down I ask how high

Now I cry again oh my God y

Did I let him in

Again and again I find myself guilty of sin

I feel too low to beg him to stay

I feel that there will be no answer when I pray

I know I know I know I have to face my fear

I have to stop being insecure

BALM

If you never face life, you are not living. We all have challenges but don't let them control your life. Deal with them and heal. Once you face the fear, you will not be without true security. Just live! Insecurities make you make bad choices. Face it head on and live with it.

PICTURE THIS

I have a question aren't you tired of sending pics
To these dudes that I think are trying to put together a quick flick
Whey they hit share, you become al loose chic
You will not be called a victim nor will he be called sick
Instead he's cool
Although it was he that broke the rules
I remember when this happened to that poor little girl in junior high school
Everybody saying how dumb she was but I said he was cruel
She thought he wanted her and she was raised to please
He convinced her that she was what he need
The whole time he was screwing her body, mind and soul
She subitys to the devil and awaits getting old
There's something wrong with this
He thinks he won because she sent the pic
But suffering in his future if he continues to play tricks
So young girl, learn from this
Get over it
Hold your head high
Now picture this

BALM

Everyone makes mistakes. Now a days technology is overwhelming. People can screenshot private conversations and more. social media has people being socially crazy. They run to the sites to hurt people instead of uplifting a society. This was a true story of a young girl who was only in junior high. She was asked to pose nude by a boyfriend. When he got upset with her, he told everyone look at this girl naked. It was devastating for her being judged by everyone around. I felt sorry for her and I had anger for the young man who thought that his actions were cool. At the end of the day, we all make mistakes. She will either hold her head up and push through to higher places or listen to negativity and be pulled into a downward spiral. She would then continue to do things on a lower level. As a community, we can be forgiving and help our youth instead of pushing them further down.

TIGHT

Tonight I lay here feeling kind of tight.
Maybe it's because I jogged earlier or the man strike
Something is going on inside of me
This aching don't seem rite
Frankly I would have preferred that life stayed put
But the one that I thought was for me
Killed the flowers by pulling up by the roots
I tried replanting them but they were already dead
So I got new ones instead
But kept expecting that they would soon be dead
Yes I gave up on life by expecting strife
Instead of smiling which was a beautiful sight
I frown a lot and stay up tight

BALM

Release the tension by taking a deep breath and letting your experiences in life go through you. If not, you will keep so much pressure built up inside of you, that your personality and your face will be tight. Breathe and smile. You got this.

MR. RIGHT

I'm feeling myself tonight
Sure wish I had Mr. Right
Youthful, beautiful ad useful is how I feel
So please let this be real
I can't believe it I'm so full of energy
From head to toe inside out I am a beauty
If you are Mr. right you can use me
As I climn my mountain I hope that he awits at my peak
Mr. right must be ready to climb high with me
The higher we climb we will see great things and some tragedies
But if you're Mr. right, you will climax with me
I'm feeling myself tonight
And before I sleep, I'm claiming my Mr. right.

BALM

This is simply coaching myself through the difficult times of loneliness to be patient. The right one will come eventually as long as you remain open.

MENTAL PAIN

That day when you become so ingulfed with pain
That yu begin to wonder when the day will come that you join the insane.
You choose to be secluded and stay in your own lane
Since every time you cry they ignore your pain
Now you thought you were doing whatever it took
To get attention by putting your thoughts on Facebook
You shared your personal feelings so that the social world will look
They can read your status
But will never be able to feel your madness
Why does she share all the sadness
Who reads attempting to not judge yet understand
Who will be there to extend a helping hand
Maybe it will take one word
To keep her from giving up
She leaves this life because it's too rough
Don't cry now you didn't read between the lines
I didn't know she was dying'
Her entire life she was always crying

BALM

There is a thin line between sane and insane. Never underestimate when a person has taken too much physical or mental pain. Even though they cry all the time, listen to them and offer to help them. Dig deep into yourself and remember when you were in a dark place. Did you seek attention? How did you handle this situation? Share your story maybe it will help.

GOD SENT YOU

Did God send you

Sometimes my mid goes crazy and I start to wonder if those church folk are guilty of fraud

They said child stop searching and wait on God

So I waited and I prayed

While I was feeling inspired you came

And not long after learning your name

I was tricked by my own mind I convinced myself that I was finally out of the game

It used to take years then it went to months now its only taking days for me to realize that you will only make me blue

So Did God send you

I have realized that when it comes to a good man there are very few

But before I continue

To let old boy do what he do

I will keep my legs closed

And we will not screw

Until I am marred and know that God Sent You

BALM

This is a beautiful message of remaining patient. Waiting on God to send you the right man. When you submit to him and stop being engulfed in a world of sin, you can discern who is right for yo

POET NOT A PROPHET

I'm a poet not a prophet
Yet everything that I've written seems to come to past
For instance, I wrote about him leaving and again it didn't last
I guess it's the curse of getting old
When you become set in your ways and every man you get must function by your remote control
Once I hit the power button
Then suddenly
There's a malfunction like what was once hard has become soft
I have the control so I turned it off
I'm a poet not a prophet
Yet I can imagine what happens tomorrow
I see the pain I see the sorrow
Maybe that is why she is old
And have to keep control
She is the one trying to keep things in tack
When she loses her remote things get all out of whack
She too old she can't withstand another heart attack
Love me and I will try to stay off your back

160

BALM

Hey Sis! Men don't like to feel like they are being controlled. We because of unfortunate circumstances, feel like we have to be in control so than we can keep the man we love. However, what we are doing is pushing him away. Take it from me, he's worth having in your life. In Islam we are taught to study your man, learn him and be his help meet. Let him use the remote.

FROZEN

Always writing rapp songs but never got rich
Workout everyday but never got fit
Body never tapered with
My age is always guessed wrong I'll always be the ish
Minus 20 they wish
I could be what's on their dish
Yes I smiled forever flattered
I got a purpose and age matters
See when you young and dumb
You may lose your mind over some
Age aint nothing but a number
But if all you offer is your lumber
I regret agreeing to communicate
When all you do is text gm every day
Never once do you say
What time shall I pick you up for our date
Once again irate
I remember why I began to hate
I slipped up and forgot about my faith
God said on me you should wait
But disobedient I refused to stop seeking because of my age I may be too late
Then I had a revelation

As I was on the phone with dude having a conversation

Be thankful that you are still getting chosen

Some of us get better with time we're Frozen

BALM

Black don't crack but her heart does. Stop being so wrapped up in looks and wait on the man who wants more than that. And since you will look young for a while just because you're black, slow down and get it right this time Sis!

RAIN

Sone get upset

They become depressed

They have no energy and feel drained

Busy explaining just why they complain

But should be busy bettering their self if they don't love who they became

As for me I'm thankful that I who used to be the same

Have accepted why God made it rain

The sun is warm and pretty all you see is the light

It's so comfortable your future looks bright

So as long as the weather is sunny you feel that everything wrong is right

So you continue to do wrong

Until everyone that loved you are gone

Oh but you don't see that because you have others surrounding you saying you are the sun

They agree with you fight

You so bright

Fun in the sun so you will never learn

If the sun always shined your skin would get burned

Now as for I grew up and stopped thinking the same

Today I'm so thankful for the rain

BALM

Don't be surprised if when your healing comes and you are thankful for life's ups and downs and you become a positive person to be around, that people who don't want to be exposed stay away from you. When all you did was gossip and brag about vain things, your phone never stopped ringing. Its ok keep being thankful for the rain in life and you will find true happiness. You will not waste energy complaining about things that out of your control. Turn on the light that shines through the rain.

A date

You can't determine my fate
I am the only one who chooses my destination. I will choose my own mate
Some lose as they listen to others with nothing to gain saying wait
This is my life
I recognize the hater's trait
Tell her what to do
While they live however they want too
Will have you believing.
While being deceiving
That they love you
And everything that they say is true
Then you refuse to move
Unless it
S to their groove
Although you know what's right
You have given up the fight
You have given up on life
Because you surrendered to strife
This no longer your life
Until, you have completely seemed to fail
When you really decide to say forget heaven I'll take hell
It is then that they will have a good old story to tell

Those same people who you thought wished you well

Wished you'd fail

Wished you out of heaven and int the pits of hell

Thank goodness they don't determine your fate

This is still your life and we all have a date

BALM

Shut off the noise of the world and focus on yourself. Love yourself and then you can trust you. Sometimes we never get comfortable with who we are, so we are always looking to others for answers. Figure your own life out because it is your only life.

BLUERYSE

Put one foot in front of the other.

Next thing I knew I was running out the gutter

Those books, songs and plays that were low had to cease

Everything I do ow I dop for God because I believe

I looked in the mirror what do I see

My name had to change cause I'm finally free

I was so blind for attention I would do any thing

Thought everything was ok trying to live my dream

Thought I had toi dress to impress with most of my body seen

But one day I learned to pray and Allah delivered a queen

Got my thoughts out the gutter

That ain't the place I want to be

It was time for my name to change I'm finally free

It's about time to Ryse from the color blue

It's hard to explain unless you've been through what I've been through

I spent so many years stuck in the energy of blue

Cried so many tears now everyone hears the blues

It's time to ryse the blues have been heard

The next energy is spirituality

Ryse go and spread the word

Blue Ryse

See the truth in my eyes

If you don’t see me in hell

Don’t act surprised

It was time for Blue to Ryse

BALM

This is a song that I wrote and recorded at the end of 2022. I used it as the conclusion because it talks about my overall healing. BlueUnique was my artist’s name for years. However, it is time that I rise. It is time to share the wisdom that I have learned on my journey.

The blue chakra represents communication. When I got to this energy level, I was happy to finally be heard. I began to sing even though I’m not the greatest singer. I would go on to release several albums under the artist’s name of BlueUnique. About six months ago, I decided that it was time for my name to change to BlueRyse. My music was more uplifting and less unique. It wasn’t until I was writing the single BlueRyse to explain the name change that I realized that I was rising out of the blue energy to the next level which is wisdom/spirituality. I will not use another color to describe the ryse but I am using Ryse to describe a Ryseclass and a Rysecast. A class on TikTok and a podcast on anchor.

CONCLUSION
STANDING ON THE MOON

I never considered my father as an issue, I put it all on my mother
So today I vow to show her how much I love her
I'm still striving to be the perfect wife but now I have more than the man
I have a plan
At one of my lowest moments, I was given a word
Words that my ears had never heard
The teachings of Elijah Muhammad from Minister Farrakhan
Words of comfort and wisdom that would help us overcome
As far as those girls
My world
The younger two lets me think I did alright
However, my oldest is still determined to fight
To her I will always be the one who ruined her life
She just said las week that she didn't understand
How her momma wasn't there to hold her hand
Another public display
Trying to humiliate
Saying that She doesn't have a mother
Making my heart suffer
But I would pray

Reflect on what does the Quran say

After difficulty there is ease

I'm different now because I believe

In staying close to God staying in the higher me

Now I have the Will

Which according to the Min. is the power of God in any human being to accomplish what you will

Studying the words of all the prophets with a God sent teacher

He's not an average preacher

He taught that no nation can rise any higher than its woman

He said that 75% of the work was with her

He said that she is the key to the kingdom of God

This beautiful black woman is more than just an average broad

He taught me that name Jerri can be rearranged to Mary

Just change the constant and the vowel

That's how

Then as a Mary, she will be humble yet wise.

She will love God with all her soul

She will listen and study on the words of her teacher

She is a determined believer

She always seeks wisdom

She will help her people escape doom

She will create old to new

With the love in her womb

She is standing on the Moon

THE END

STANDING ON THE MOON

172

CONTACT ME

@ heavenismine9@gmail.com or bluedealsheals.com

www.ingramcontent.com/pod-product-compliance
Lightning Source LLC
LaVergne TN
LVHW050547160826
845677LV00011B/2215

* 9 7 9 8 3 7 5 0 2 7 0 8 1 *